CW00645843

PAGE NUMBERS OF CHAPTERS

1
WELCOME

It's often said by people exclaiming the love of their own profession, that it is "the most fun you can have with your clothes on". Unfortunately, considering the career of a voice over artist, we cannot boast such a claim, as rustling clothing and very sensitive microphones do not make a good mix. And it does get awfully hot in our little voice booths. So quite often, those clothes do have to come off! But if you share my love of being able to give consistently high-quality audio performances from a variety of types of script, using nothing more than acting skills, flexibility and the power of the human voice, then this book is for you.

First of all, I really hope that you're not going to be disappointed by this book. Over the years in various bookshops, I have flicked through and bought many titles about the voiceover business and have been terribly deflated finding that the author just really wanted to tell their readers all about how they got their big break meeting some top agent in an elevator in LA, or all about their personal life in great detail or about some obscure awards they'd won. Of course, none of that would be relevant to anyone who just wanted to know solid practical techniques and proven working tips that would help them in their careers as successful voice artists themselves.

So, I make you this promise, that after this short section, I'm not going to talk about myself at all, apart from things that I have personally do that may help you in some way. I've tried my best to cram in as much useful information as possible about the voiceover business and recording and editing techniques that would be useful to someone who has just set up, or is ready to take their voice career to the next level.

I'll go through the opportunities out there and how to grasp them, how to optimise your website and showreels, how to give realistic quotes and quality customised demos. You'll also get detailed practical tips on all sorts of things that can make your life easier and to enjoy your life more. There are even sections on dealing with difficult clients, long-form projects like audiobooks and the threat of AI. But first – let's get me out the way, shall we?

My first job was in 1975 at the biggest commercial radio station in the UK outside of London, called Piccadilly Radio, based in the city of Manchester. As well as presenting programmes, I also worked in the commercial production department, where, I recorded voiceovers for adverts and promos, and also "taped" (yes, we had reel-to-reel "tape recorders" back then) various actors and voice over artists who would come in to our studios to read their scripts. They had to physically come in, we had no internet then of course, and I would mix their voice tracks with sound effects and music off vinyl disc (no, we had no CD's either!) or tape cartridge.

Legal commercial radio had just started in the UK (after the 1960's pirate radio ships) and we were really beginners in the world of voiceover work and commercial production, so I was packed off to New York for a spell to spend time round various talk and music radio stations and production studios to see how they did things. America had had commercial radio since the 1920's, so they knew all about writing and producing quality and powerful adverts and promos. I learnt some great techniques that we could adapt to the UK market and recorded voiceovers as well over in NYC in my British voice and learnt to perform various Mid-Atlantic accents!

After Piccadilly Radio, I worked for the BBC television in the 80's as a News presenter and a features reporter and later in the 90's ran a TV motoring channel at Granada TV, a commercial TV station. But throughout all my full-time jobs, I have always been regularly recording voice scripts. There's been hardly a day in my working life where I haven't recorded some kind of voice over of some kind.

In the late 90's, I decided to go fully freelance, take advantage of the internet revolution and built a booth and studio at home, where things just rocketed for me. I can honestly say that in the last 15 years, I have regularly earned about triple what I was bringing in even as a staff executive at that TV station.

Plus, I'm working for myself, I work mostly from home, and there aren't many outgoings. After all, once you've set your studio up, your main outgoings are simply on internet and power charges, software and website subscriptions, accountant's fees and of course a tax bill every year. That's it really. After all, there are only so many microphones you can buy in life! I also personally don't have an exclusive agent to pay out a percentage to for every job either! But more on agents later.

So in this book, I hope to offer to you my 40 years plus of experience in all the many different facets of the life of a professional voiceover and I hope that you grow your success like I have too.

2
HOW THE NET OFFERED VOICEOVERS THE WORLD

I almost wasn't going to write this chapter, until a friend of mine I've been helping set up his own voice studio at home, told me that his marketing efforts to get voice over work had started with organisations local to where he lived. And I couldn't quite understand why he was doing this, as he didn't actually know anyone there and also these companies didn't have audio studios. Yes of course, make good relationships with local recording studios, where you may physically go into from time to time, but when it comes to potential clients, the internet has opened up the complete planet to us all, and home studio working is now so easy.

As I mentioned in the welcome section, when I first started my voice career in the 70's, actors had to physically turn up at studios to record scripts. It was extremely rare to do anything "down the line". If a specific required voice actor couldn't make it to your studio, you would have to book audio lines days or weeks in advance, and quality audio line bookings would be very expensive.

So, a group of voice artists and actors would literally tour the country continuously, staying in cheap hotels or even sleeping in their cars to save cash, and then knocking at the doors of radio stations in that city the next day to ask if there were any suitable scripts in the commercial production department's "in" trays!

It was a very hard life for the freelance voiceover back in the 70's and 80's. These people didn't even have mobile phones, so had to find phone boxes or cadge the use of radio station office telephones to see if anyone had booked them via various concierge services. Today, it doesn't matter where you live. Create a **.com** website as a shopwindow and the world is yours!

You know, some say that you have to get lucky breaks in our business to be successful, but remember the old adage, "the harder you work, the luckier you get". My job in writing this book is to help you channel your hard work in the right direction so you can reap as much "luck" as you want on the journey.

Please feel free to flip round the sections you're interested in; it's not like a novel where all is revealed at the end! I hope you'll find this book useful for you.

WHY WE'RE LUCKY!

Lucky that the internet connects us all together so we can be directed by someone the other side of the planet with virtually no delay or extra costs.

Lucky that broadband speeds are forever getting faster and more stable.

Lucky that digital technology can provide incredible quality audio equipment at very affordable prices so we can set up home studios without breaking the bank.

Lucky that developers have created solutions to make remote direction easier for us voiceovers such as Source Connect, ipDTL, Riverside, Cleanfeed and so on.

Lucky we can be paid instantly via PayPal or Bank transfer and not having to physically pay in those pesky "cheques" at banks.

Lucky that English is an international language, and if somebody wants an English language voice over recording, they're not going to care where you are physically located, they just want to know they are going to get a good professional job, recorded properly.

Lucky that media creation is expanding, and voice artists of all types are in demand.

3
EXCLUSIVE AGENT OR INDEPENDENT?

When you're starting out, you really need to decide which voiceover "camp" you wish to be in. The two camps are best explained as "voiceover artist with exclusive agent" and "independent, with various non-exclusive agents". We're all different types of people, with different talents and connections, and some voiceover artists are better suited to one camp than the other.

First of all, if you have an agent with an "exclusive" deal, this means that if you're approached directly by a client, such as an advertising agency, production company, or even a direct end-client to record and to edit a voiceover script, under the terms of your arrangement, you would have to refer them to your agent, and not discuss any details of the fee or even if you'd actually do the job. You'd say the catchphrase: "Call my agent!"

You'd also not be generally allowed to post your services on voiceover directory sites or so called "Pay To Play" sites like Voices.com, Bodalgo, Voice 123 and so on. If you have your own website, the only contact numbers and emails will those of your agent – only! If you get direct calls, you'd refer all job enquiries to your agent. In return, your exclusive agent would promise to try and get work for you, and to negotiate the best fees for you. However, there would be no guarantee of any work at all.

So what are the advantages of having an exclusive deal with a voiceover agent? Well, it saves you any hassle dealing with bookings and invoicing, and your agent will know other potential and confirmed bookings for you, so nothing gets double booked and also you won't have issues recording scripts for rival brands in the same sector which can cause real problems.

The other major advantage is that you may find it difficult to put a decent fee on your services, so your agent will be able to negotiate for you often an amount far more than you would maybe have dared to suggest, so even with the agent's commission, you still earn more on that job. This fee negotiation isn't often that important for basic non-broadcast narration, corporate films or internet promos and so on. For these types of basic script, most fees are pretty similar for similar script duration and type, but good agents can negotiate high fees for TV and radio commercial use using every trick in the book if an advertising agency really wants your voice for a project. Agents can also chase extra payments if your voiceover recordings are used for longer than in the original agreement.

Voiceovers with exclusive agents tend to be based in cities, as this arrangement works best for bookings in recording studios, and often voiceovers with exclusive agents don't have a studio of their own or aren't that technically inclined. Some agents do try and persuade their voiceovers to have a recording facility of their own, even a basic one, just to record basic custom mp3 demos they can send off, but there are many who don't have a studio at all, and actually never want to do anything technical, which can work out fine for some, but for others they will find that this will put a big dent in their earning potential, as they won't be able to record custom demos for jobs unless they go to a studio, eating up precious time and somebody has to pay that studio bill.

So, I think you'll see that for a voiceover who is maybe a jobbing actor or has another full-time job in a city and is trying to get a start in the world of voiceovers, having an exclusive agent to source and to get you work is a highly attractive option. Especially if it seems that they are going to do all the marketing for you! But of course, it's not as simple as that.

You will need to persuade the agent to take you on in the first place, and with an agent, you don't just simply sit back and wait for the phone to ring, you'll need to do your part as well, and more on this later.

You don't HAVE to live in a big city near lots of recording studios to have an exclusive arrangement with a voice-over artist. Quite a few of the big names I know live in the middle of nowhere, but they do need to be technically proficient with their own broadcast quality studio. Plus, for urgent jobs, they need to be able to drop everything to get to an in – person session at a recording studio.

So, I think you are getting the idea, that this type of voice-over, is more of an actor-type person, or even a sort of existing "celebrity", who has got an exclusive agent to do most of the marketing, to sort out recording sessions and to invoice and chase the cash afterwards. Generally speaking, these sessions would be well paid and worthwhile to travel to a physical session in a recording studio that's not your own. An agent wouldn't be interested in the smaller jobs, because the hassle of setting them up and doing the extra work needed, would not justify the small amount of percentage the agent would get, especially if re-takes were needed.

So, would you as a newcomer to the voice-over world, be able to secure an agent? Well, that's all up to your talent, your connections, and whether maybe you are a bit of a celebrity already. There are many actors who are already quite established on the stage or doing TV work, who have never really thought of doing voice-over work, and they'd be naturals at doing it....maybe you're one of these people. In this sort of situation, because you have a bit of a "name", it should be fairly easy to get a voice agent, either an individual, or an established voice agency in the city where you are based, to represent you.

Don't automatically think, by the way, that your existing "acting" agent would be skilled at getting you voice work, as they may not have the contacts or knowledge about what specific skills or parameters are required, or anything about the rates and deals relating to voice artists. So, in this case, you'd need an agent or agency who would represent you solely and exclusively for voiceover work and nothing else, and you'd need to square it with your acting agent – saying that you wish to be represented by a "voiceover only" exclusive agent. Don't let your acting agent find out by hearing your voice on a TV spot, unless you want some ugly scenes or a nasty phone call!

So, if you are getting an exclusive voice agent under an exclusive relationship, what is the point learning more about the business from me? Well, as well as learning the essential techniques to be a first-class professional voice artist in the recording booth, you need to be able to know that your agent is doing everything they should be doing to get you work, but more importantly, one day you might like to break out and become an independent voice-over.

This has been my own situation, where I once had an exclusive agent for many years, and then when that agency closed through no fault of my own, I simply tried to see if I could make it as an independent. I was remarkably successful, and I honestly made far more income as I did with an agent representing me. It was also to me much more fun, and I felt much more in control of my own destiny. So did that mean I had a pretty bad agent? No not at all. It's simply that I realised that I am a sort of person who actually suits being an independent voice-over.

A summary. For people who are in full-time work and don't have time to commit to doing their own recording, editing and marketing, and have managed to get an agent on an exclusive basis, they may get two or three really well-paid jobs in a week, and need to travel to recording studios. They still need to have a handle on marketing, to ensure that their own agent is on the ball, and be prepared to suggest new voice showreels or voice characters for video games and so on, you have still to be active in looking for opportunities and assisting your agent.

But the other side of the coin is the life of the independent voice-over. These people are generally the types of people who like to get out there and promote their own services, and generally have the time to do it. It's not a case that the independent voice-over just doesn't want to pay any agent fees, it's because that they genuinely enjoy the variety of smaller to medium-sized jobs that come in to their email in-box each day. They like being busy. Plus, usually the independent voice-over actually enjoys the studio work, recording, shaping sound and editing. I know I do! Nothing is more frustrating to me personally, then going to a big recording studio in London, and working under an engineer who maybe is a bit slow or doesn't conduct the recording session as I would do myself. But that's just me! I happen to have been brought up with a technical mind and even as a kid, I was building little recording studios and radio transmitters! (I'm sad to admit)

So, if you want to be an independent voice-over, or you have to be because you just cannot find an agent who is willing to take you on at this stage in your career, then you will need to do all your own marketing, get an invoicing system set up and be organised with a "business head" on. You will also of course need to build a home studio or do a deal with a local friend who you can share facilities with, learn some technical skills of recording and editing your material. It is honestly not as scary as it may look, and today's software is quite easy to get used to.

If you need help, I have various video-based courses on **VoiceoverMasterclass.com** all about how to set up a voice over studio and how to do basic and intermediate audio editing with Adobe Audition software which is the industry standard.

Another advantage of being an independent voice-over, with your presence all round the world on various websites, and with your own personal website, is that you get a huge VARIETY of work each day, as well as having rarely a day without any jobs. In fact, it's a relief when you DON'T have jobs come in, to have time free to do the accounts and invoicing, and to see the family!

But as with any freelance life, psychologically, when you get a whole day without any jobs coming in at all, you sometimes get this awful feeling that the whole world doesn't want you or needs you anymore. It often isn't the case like this at all, but if you get lots of smaller jobs to keep you busy and then this is peppered with some really decent big jobs over the week, you are kept busy and you continually have that feeling that you are in demand.

The world of the voice-over is very much supply and demand, and if you go the route of having an exclusive voice agent, you may have a wonderful agent, who is trying very hard for you, and gets you to audition for all sorts of things, but you don't happen to get the actual jobs in the end. It can be very frustrating, and sometimes you will go for weeks without any paying job at all.
So let me tell you more about what type of person this second breed of VO is...an independent voiceover, like myself. This is somebody who may have many connections with various voice agencies, not just in their city or country, but round the world.

You would not be under any exclusive agreement with anybody. You would be on the websites of many agencies around the world, with voice samples and a photo as if you were working just for them, but of course, you are not, as you'll have non-exclusive arrangements! Some of these web-based voice agencies will ask you to use a false name on their site, or you'll not be allowed even a photo and you'll be just a code number on their site to identify you. That's fine, just play their game, you'll still get paid and it won't harm your other work!

As an independent voice-over, you would also of course have your own personal website, featuring audio voice samples and also videos and TV commercials that have you featured as a voiceover, and unlike your own site when represented exclusively with an agent, you'll have email and phone contact numbers direct to you. You may also be enrolled on various other voice directory websites; some of which you would pay to subscribe to, some of which would be free. More details of the best of these sites are in the section at the end. These sites would all have their different systems, and fee structures, and you may not hear from some of them for weeks or months, but then suddenly a very decent job comes in, so it's worth being on as many as them as is practicable.

So would any of these jobs for the directory-type sites be well paid, like the big city advertising agency funded jobs? Maybe, but usually they will all be small to medium-sized jobs, say between 50 and 100 dollars per script, but over time, an independent voice-over who markets themselves well, will be able to get regular work from all the various income sources.

All the small jobs add up, and we'll do some maths later on to determine income values you could attain.

To be honest, you will find as an independent, most of your income will come, not from being on voice websites with loads of other voices as competition, but from the solid relationships you will make with studios and producers who will hire you directly and regularly and will not even think of auditioning anyone else for your type of voice.

We'll all be different, but with my own contacts over the years, I make about 60% of my income from direct clients, with 40% from agencies and studios, and the "Pay to play" websites like Voices.com and also the free voice directory VO sites like FiverrPro. Then you get long term projects such as huge eLearning and audiobook projects that also are essentially direct.

4
SKILLS REQUIRED FOR VOICEOVER SUCCESS

Skill 1 - The voice itself

I'm sometimes asked by people outside the business what EXTRA skills are needed by a voice over artist. They say "Extra", because they seem to think that you just simply need to have a "nice voice". On asking what they mean by "nice", it transpires what they really mean is when it comes to, say, a British voice, someone that sounds like they're reading the news on BBC Radio 4. Sigh....

But of course, that's not actually the case at all. I know many voice artists making a really decent income, capitalising on their original regional or ethnic accents, or they have the flexibility to be able to perform many kinds of character voices, so they're more of a "voice actor", than a "voiceover". That's absolutely fine. And I know quite a few people who are brilliant at sounding "normal", just like a "man or woman in the street" and for some voice artists, that's strangely hard to do, as once you get into the groove of thinking like what a voiceover "should" sound like on many radio and TV ads, you just can't do "normal" without really struggling!

So the first skill, isn't really a skill at all, because often you just have to be yourself, and that's why virtually anybody can work in the voice business and be successful; you just have to find the clients who are looking for a voice like your natural voice or one that you can create, building on your natural voice. It really is astonishing how many different voices you can find within you when you lose your inhibitions and just try some variations out.

You won't be great at them all, nobody is. But I bet after some hours trying things out with the techniques I go into later with character voices, that you'll magically discover a list of new sounds, accents and characters that you never thought you could achieve before.

Skill 2 – Sightreading

Yes, you DO have to be proficient in the language you are recording in. Otherwise, you will be forever tripping up and leaving gaps, and it will take ages for you to edit after your recording. so, sightreading is an essential skill for voiceovers. You can see how good you are by picking up a random newspaper or book, flicking it open and just starting to read anywhere at reasonable speed of 150 words per minute, and not making any mistakes.

Pretend you're being recorded, and you mustn't leave any gaps, or trip up anywhere. The trick is that while your mouth is reading a set of words, your eyes need to look ahead to find any "danger" words , maybe a name that you're not sure how it's pronounced so your brain can start thinking of this while you are still speaking. Then your ears need to monitor what you're saying to make sure it is accurate. It IS very possible; more on all this later.

Skill 3 - Timing

One of my party tricks was being able to judge exactly the duration of 30 seconds without looking at a watch or clock, because I had recorded so many 30 seconds radio and TV commercials, and there seems to be a sort of an internal clock in my head. Maybe it's the voiceover equivalent of having perfect pitch in a musician!

This particular skill isn't essential, but you do need to have a sense what pace is, so for example, if you are on a directed session, and the director asks you to speed up a little for the next "take", you will know what you had recorded before in terms of your delivery speed, and you'd be able to shave a small part off it.

For many voiceover scripts, exact timing isn't actually that essential, but if you are recording commercials or are replacing a non-English narration of a video, then every split-second counts. In fact you may get a timed script with each paragraph or even sentence given with the exact duration required.

As time goes on, and you get more experienced, you will be able to judge exactly how long durations are, and also you'll be able to compensate for the fact that you will be able to cut out breaths afterwards if necessary. So even though you may not have an inherent good sense of timing to begin with, after a while, with many recordings under your belt, you will no doubt develop this skill to a high level.

Skill 4 – Accurate Self-Monitoring
An essential skill when you are working on your own, is to be able to monitor yourself, and I go into this in much more detail in a later section.

If it's just you who is checking how accurate you are with the words and how close the performance is to what the client has asked of you, then you need to be very strict with yourself, as if there was a producer looking over your shoulder or who is sat in an imaginary control room next door.

Yes, it can be lonely working on your own as a voiceover in your home studio, especially when you have got many self-directed scripts to do. That's why if you are not that good at self-directing, you need to try to angle your marketing to get the kinds of jobs which do have the need for a director calling the shots over your headphones.

Skill 5 – Technical skills

Technical skills are pretty essential, because unless you learn how to record and edit everything yourself, a big chunk of your wages will be going out to your engineer or audio editor. I do know a couple of people who are terribly technophobic, but great voice actors, and they've just have never had any yearning to learn the technical side of their job, and would rather have someone else do it all. But they're happy in their work, and they don't mind paying an outside studio to do the technical work for them.

If the idea of grappling with software and technology fills you with dread, and you think this is an option for you, be aware that not only will you lose money you earn sharing it with someone else, but you will not optimise all the work you can possibly get, as quite often voice work has the tendency of creating urgent projects at very unsociable hours, when most commercial studios are shut.

Skill 6- Patience

Patience is a skill that you'll need when dealing with some clients. On a directed session, where you are in an external studio or in your home booth wearing headphones, you may be reading the same 10 second line over and over and over, as various agency people on your headphones chip in with their own thoughts of how you should say the words, and quite often, they end up selecting the very first take you recorded anyway! Grrr!!

Even if you know you are right and the clients are wrong, and even if you believe there is a far better way of doing the job, unless you are specifically asked for your opinion, just button your lip and do what they ask you to do!

Sometimes, you will be directed by a production company who have had the script from the end direct client, and sometimes there's some pretty poor English in it. So, you can point this out if you like, although I have known occasions where the production company was too scared to change their client's script, and I reluctantly had to read the bad English. But a situation like this can sometimes work in your favour, when they have to ask you that to record it again, and you get paid another fee!

Skill 7 - Flexibility
Flexibility - not in voice style, but in your time. Especially if you get clients in countries in other time zones than your own one, you will need to be prepared to get up early or go to bed late, but it's fun talking to people from other countries in different parts of the planet, and you really feel that you are literally a man or woman of the world.

So these are the main skills I think a voice over should have, but there are also loads of different techniques that you will need to use for various projects in the future, and to be honest, you never stop learning. That's what makes this job so challenging and rewarding at the same time.

Skill 8 – Life experience in communication
If you've ever done business presentations or "tool talks" to colleagues at work, done any teaching work or are a parent where you communicate regularly with your kids and teach them things, all these basic human communication skills are needed to be a great voice artist. In fact, why not replace the term "voice artist" with the word "communicator". That is a far more accurate description of what your job entails.

To prove this point, go to YouTube and watch a Ted Talk or TedX Talk. Often you will be totally enthralled and sucked in to the presentations even on subjects you may not have an interest in. But often these great communicators haven't a traditionally "good" voice for voiceover work, yet the passion and nuances of their presentation, the pauses and emphasis words that all come naturally to them, add up to a very strong form of communication.

5
YOUR VOICEOVER WEBSITE

As a voiceover, it is extremely important to have a decent shop window, in other words a website aimed at potential new direct clients who can hear your voice. Existing clients that you have will rarely look back at your site once they start working with you as they will already have a relationship with you, and will ask you directly for new and updated showreels and so on. They could send the link to others like their direct clients who are choosing voices for a new campaign.

They could initially find your website through good Google SEO or just by luck – or much more likely from a link from you on an email when you are doing your marketing or from other people who may recommend you.

Your website needs to be very functional. If you go on a website and it looks like it was done in the 1990s with an "Enter website" button, and the computer still needs Flash to play your audio or video files, (not even supported by Adobe anymore) or you can't download the showreels, would you be impressed?

But don't go down the route of "style over substance" with big arty photos like many advertising and creative agencies do. Yes, your brand and image ARE important, but first and foremost, potential new clients need to see that you're a professional. It needs to have a clean and clear layout and users need to have quick access to your demos and showreels. It needs to be very obvious where to click to hear your voice, without any scrolling too much or looking up menus. Your contact details should be very bold and obvious to find.

I'm not claiming my own voiceover website will win any awards for style or design, but it's very functional. Every square inch has a use. After a lot of tweaking, it has been very efficient for years as my own *"shop window"*. I know it's not a great site, but as Oscar Wilde said, *"A work of art is never completed, merely abandoned"*. No apologies, I've honestly just been too busy with real well-paid work to find time to update it, and there's only one little ol' me. You're welcome to adapt the layout for your own needs if you like. I designed and built my own voice website at **EnglishVoice.tv** using **www.WIX.com**

If you can, it's best if you DO make it yourself, as web designers never make it EXACTLY as you'd like it to look like, and they will often charge for just the slightest of extra essential updates that would take you just a minute of your time.

Choose a domain that is search engine friendly for voiceovers and it MUST be **.com**; no matter where you live on the planet, as a voice artist, you are a man or woman of the world now, it will help you enormously to .com your site and not be stuck with one that identifies your country. There is nothing wrong with having multiple domains that all go to your main site, and this is easy to set up on WIX.com too; you can have 5 switches as part of your WIX Premium account.

All the main features for a voiceover need to be on the home page. It has my name and photo so people can see immediately my sex and approximate age I am along with my contact details and there is a hyperlink on the email address. Please don't have a separate "Contact" page that people have to find. And do not have a silly fill-in form, with "Click to show you're human" boxes and "click the pictures with mail boxes" - people hate these things! You won't get spammed out with just your email on your site, if you get a few just select them and assign them spam or phishing so you'll never see them again.

If you haven't a clue how to design a website, WIX have loads of great templates and you can simply replace the photos and text and add in loads more audio players and download links. Or hire a WIX designer on Fiverr.com or Upwork.com. Once it's all done and you're happy, then change the log in password and you now can update it yourself in the future.

Find other voiceover sites and admire ones you like and get really angry at ones you don't. Actually, this "angry" element I find has led to a lot of success for me in my life. For example, if I hear a voiceover, watch a video or visit a website that I think is awful, I get angry! I think, "Grrr...! I could do better than that!" That gives me real impetus to better what I have seen or heard!

You may notice on my own website that there are various versions of the main details of my homepage in other languages. Even though I don't speak or record in these other languages, I get an awful lot of work from people who want English versions of existing videos in their native language. So as a simple courtesy to them, I explain a bit about myself and how I work, in their own home language when they click the button.

My website has 32 (at the time of writing) different showreels – more about these later, but there's a clear link where people can download all of them as mp3's for their casting files.

Plus, on the home page there's a variety of TV ads with my voice on that I have sucked off YouTube, Vimeo, etc., (with Wondershare AllMyTube software) or have been given directly to me from clients. These videos I host on my own personal Vimeo channel and embed them into my website, in case any ads are deleted from the other original platforms.

You can of course make a collection of your own radio and TV ads you have made; once they are broadcast they are in the public domain so you don't have to ask the ad agency to put them on your site, although sometimes they would appreciate a credit caption. However, the point of your site is to show your voice off at its best, and if your voice is mixed with other actors on the ad or drowned in awful music that is so loud that your voice can't be heard clearly, then don't bother – just create a showreel of this type or even use the same script yourself!

I have a (non-Autoplay) video on my "about" page with some clips from various ads, which is nice to have, but not essential for a starter in the VO business. It's just that I also offer "in-vision" recordings as I have a mini TV studio at home with teleprompter, so it shows my work off here too, and there's a separate page for in-vision, rates, character voices, and eLearning.

So what about SEO, or Search Engine Optimisation? I personally think that you'll get far more work by doing solid direct marketing (discussed later) and using the website as a place to send people to find out more; you'll get far more work doing this than hoping people will type in the word "voiceover" into Google and finding you on page one; this just isn't going to happen. But SEO as much as you can for free and it won't take you long to basically optimise your website.

Find relevant keywords for your services, there are plenty of free ones on the net. Look at the keyword density in your text, and regularly post relevant voiceover articles somewhere on your site, even just short ones, as long as the articles are linked via the home page menu. This is so important.

Maybe you make YouTube videos with tips and advice for other voice people, or how to do accents, or anything like that – and you should- we should all help each other; then paste the transcript on a page in your website and ensure it's linked to the home page.

You can also answer questions on Reddit or Facebook groups where you can be useful to others and offer a link to your articles on your website.

For any graphics or photos on your site, don't forget your tags! Right click on photos and graphics in your website editor and call the photo something relevant with dashes (hyphens) and not underscores. " **Jhy4567733.jpg**" or whatever means <u>nothing</u> to the Google crawler 'bots. So a photo of you in your booth could be renamed in its metadata: **"Firstname-LastName-Broadcast-Quality-Studio"** or something relevant.

Make sure your name is fully <u>consistent</u> throughout your site. So First name and Last name, always. Or just your voice nickname throughout. Be consistent.

If you have a particular skill or type of voice, then major on this. If, for example, you have a totally authentic Bronx accent or Liverpool accent, then put this in your keywords and even on the text on your site but of course also mention, if it's true, that you are flexible for other voice styles and accents as well.

It's a big mistake that rookie voiceovers make when they enrol on various voiceover directory sites to tick every little box of the accents and talents and job types that they can offer. They think that that will give them more work, but this strategy can really backfire. Answer really honestly and play to your strengths.
You need to update your website regularly, even if it's just a few minor weekly tweaks to help Google 'bots know it's an active concern, so it'll push you higher in the rankings.

What about Social Media? You absolutely must have a LinkedIn account and update this as much as you do with your main website, with plenty of links to your site.   Invite as many useful people as you can to be part of your network, such as producers, directors, audio and video studios, head of talents, game company staff, and so on. Sometimes LinkedIn allows you to invite a bulk load of people to your network, but don't just "select all".

Think carefully - who might be useful to you and be interested in your work? Then make sure what you post is relevant and interesting. Does it pass the "Have you seen this fascinating and useful article" test?

I would not recommend bothering with Facebook as it's not a business social media platform, however, Twitter is useful for being on if only so you can follow various companies who sometimes post job opportunities on there. Video game companies in particular use Twitter in this way.

TOP VOICEOVER WEBSITE TIPS:

- **Try to look at your "finished" website from the point of view of a casting director, production company boss and a direct end-client. Would they be impressed?**

- **Check that you haven't left the "title" of the site or home page as "HOME". Call it your name or "Showreels" Your name and the words voiceover, voice talent, voice artist, voice actor should be peppered throughout the text on the pages of your site, but make sure the home page is clean and has the basic details and your showreels / TV ads if appropriate.**

- Check it all looks OK and works fine on a) Widescreen laptops/computers b) 4:3 aspect ratio "Squarer" laptops/computers and c) Mobile phones

- Make sure it is very easy to download your showreels as mp3 files.

- Set up a professional email address that matches your website. Don't use amateur looking and old "Hotmail" addresses. For example if your website is HarryBananaVoiceover.com, **then** mail@harrybananavoiceover.com **is fine.**

- The three main things people are looking for with a voiceover are a) Your sex b) Your age c) Your natural accent d) Where you live   Are these clear on your site?

- Is your photo up to date and professional-looking, that is not arty, zany or blurred?

- Is your name 100% consistent on the website, the SEO tags and on the names of the showreel files? Is your name on the domain name, or at least on your email address?

- Make contact details very clear with email hyperlinks and not an annoying form to fill in which is even harder on a phone.

6

CREATING SHOWREELS

If you're starting out in the voice business, and you've already invested time in learning the business from books like mine, and have invested money in equipment, why would you not want to also invest in hiring a professional showreel producer to create your first reels?

You may have heard horror stories that not all of them are that good, and many of them are very expensive, and maybe you're convinced that surely you'll know best what you're good at, right? But the truth is that a good showreel producer will hear things in your voice that you won't have noticed. Some elements or nuances that could be further developed to turn you from good to excellent.

After creating your first showreels, and understanding more about what you can and cannot perform, and what you could go on to improve, you will develop a good ear yourself, as this is of course essential when you're self-directing real jobs without your demo producer by your side.

If you aren't employing the services of a professional demo producer, then I suggest you team up with another voice artist, maybe one that isn't a rival to you, for example someone of the opposite sex or of a far different age. Play them your showreels and ask them to give you good honest feedback. Then you would offer to give them feedback on their own showreels, and where they could improve them. This "buddy" system has been found to be useful for many voiceovers starting out and needing a peer review system that's practical and inexpensive.

I'm a big fan of making lots of showreels that are aimed at not just specific voice styles, but also aimed to specific industries or applications as well. So if you have a client who is looking for someone to voice, for example, a medical narration, then you can actually offer an example of you reading an actual medical narration. It may actually be virtually exactly the same voice style, accent and speed as your "nature documentary" showreel, but that's not important; you need to give confidence to the potential client, that you can deliver exactly what they want. Not just the voice style, but in dealing with the subject matter, pronouncing correctly complex medical terms and all!

You need to create a list of all the voice styles that you are confident of pulling off well. And I mean WELL. Cross off the list anything that you really are not proud of. Use the "50 jobs" list in the appendix if you like, to get you started. This might include your "natural" voice in your native accent or corporate narration, fast and enthusiastic style, hard sell commercials, award ceremony type announcements, informative phone prompts, character voices from zany professor to beach bum to Santa...whatever...just keep that list going, and then you can divide it up into different categories to give yourself the best chance of being selected when people find your website, or you direct them to it, and they play the relevant showreels.

But I'll say this again. Be hard with yourself. If your heart isn't into doing some elements, don't do them. If your shouty "Hard Sell" voice sounds desperate, or your Welsh accent is a bit ropey, just forget it. Concentrate on what you can perform well at the moment; you can always add to your skills and your showreels later.

Of course, a showreel, even using real recordings from your work, only shows what you did for someone else and they were pleased with, and not what you can do for the specific new client. When you are contacted by a potential new client, don't just direct them to your website, but <u>always</u> offer to record a custom demo, recording a part of the actual script that they want recorded. You would do this for free of course, and it vastly improves your chance of being selected for that particular job.

If you're starting out with no real jobs recorded yet, just simply make script extracts up. Clients care about your voice and performance, not the content. They really don't. If you aren't good at writing scripts, there are plenty of websites where you can get inspiration, even **Voices.com** have got a section where you can take sample scripts and adapt them for your own use, you don't even have to be a subscriber. It's not as if you are trying to impress the listener with big names that you have worked for,(this really is NOT important and it's best never to brag, although it can be effective if agents do it on your behalf) they just want to hear your voice style, and how you handle each type of script.

When you are making showreels, make two versions. One without music in the background, and one with. It gives more authenticity and mood to have music on showreels, as long as the music is mixed low and doesn't drown your wonderful voice! I tend to keep the music ones on my website, but often a client will need a version without any music at all, so they can try out your voice with a particular music track they have selected for a specific project. So be organised and keep these "non-music" versions where you know you can find them.

Don't make showreels too long, about 60 to 90 seconds is perfectly enough to give people an idea of what you can do. Don't leave your best material to the end. Many people flicking through various showreels may only listen to the first 10 or 20 seconds.

TOP SHOWREEL TIPS:

- Only give showreels that show off your very best types of voices that match your age, sex and natural accent. Don't pretend you can do everything. Be really good at what you know you can do well.

- Don't just think advertising showreels, visitors to your site may need a audiobook producer or a documentary narrator.

- Every line counts. You don't have to read full scripts in one take; take your time and perfect each line; in fact in the final compilation, it's often best if you edit together the best sentences from all your recordings.

- Never say your name ("a slate") at the start of every showreel. If you do, Agents then have the hassle of editing these names off when they pitch for big gigs when they fear clients or production companies will bypass them and find you direct; they sometimes give us "codenames" or "numbers" when they pitch us for huge jobs. The file name however, should ALWAYS include your name, and that's easy for agents to alter.

- Don't just think "voiceover" or "announcer" – the trend in radio and TV ads in particular are now for much more natural sounding voices and accents. Do at least one showreel in your completely natural and "normal" voice, without any of the affected attributes that traditionally voiceovers have been asked to perform with.

7
WHAT TO CHARGE?
RATE CARDS AND QUOTES

When you're setting up your voiceover business, you need to determine what to charge people. You're exchanging your time and your talents and the use of your equipment for money, and some types of recording and editing work take longer than others.

But, uniquely to the voiceover world, WHERE your voice ends up determines the fee as well. The recording and editing may take you exactly the same time, but if your recording is for a network TV commercial, it pays more than a cinema commercial, and that pays more than a network radio spot and that pays more than a regional radio spot and more than a phone prompt. Why is that?

Well, it's a historical reason that involves unions and various individuals that I won't bore you with now, but it's all about the amount of "ears" that will eventually hear your voice. In fact, a network TV ad played once may not pay as much as if it were played hundreds of times. Should you worry about this? Let's say there were two TV commercials being produced, the first using a few graphics and copyright free music for local TV with a production budget of $1,000, and another with big name actors, filmed on location with a Red Arrows jet flypast and music composed by Andrew Lloyd Webber with a total budget of $2 million.

Even though it took you the same time to do the voiceover part, wouldn't you want a bigger slice of that much bigger pie? 'nuff said. For jobs on voiceover directory sites and the so called "Pay To Play" subscription sites, the fees usually will already be determined.

But if a client comes direct to you and asks for a quote, what do you say? First of all you need to determine a "rate list" or so called "rate card" for your own services.

It wasn't that long ago when us voiceovers determined rates for various durations of script for so-called "non-broadcast" use. This meant no radio use, no television use, and no cinema use. Any other use, including the internet would be fine. But of course, this is crazy, as a small engineering firm in Poland may need you for a YouTube video that will be seen by 500 people, and a huge global brand may need you for a social media campaign on Facebook or YouTube that will be seen by millions.

So calling "the internet" non-broadcast these days is of course, nonsense. You really need to guesstimate the amount of people who will hear your voice. A good agent will be able to work this out quickly, but as you are your own agent, you really have to guess and not be greedy!

From this guessing you'd create a basic rate card, but not all scripts are equal. If you need to correct badly translated English, adhere to fixed exact timings on the script or constantly look up the pronunciation of non-English names that eats up recording AND editing time, you need to add something on to compensate for this.

Google "Voiceover rates" and you'll find many guides put out by organisations and unions that detail voiceover rates. When I say "detail" there is so much detail it is often very confusing, and to be honest, impractical. There are some voiceover websites who take care of this pesky quoting money stuff for you.

For example, **VoiceRealm.com** have fixed fees that are quite fair, and they have the resources and time to check if the voiceover recording is being used more after the agreed time paid for. You, as a busy independent voice talent, won't have time to do any of this, I assure you. For example, did I have the resources and time to check if my CMV Cruise ads were still being run in Australia after a year? No, I did not. But Voices.com did, and the client actually wanted an extension and paid both of us again for another year of use.

If an agent – and I have 5 non-exclusive agents around the world - asks me to do a job, the fee is always divided into two sections, the "session" fee that pays for you to record the script(s) and that's it, and then the usage fee is on top.

For high end jobs, quite often a selection of voice actors are booked and paid to record a full hour or two of directed sessions, and then they edit every voice into the adverts or animations or whatever before they make their mind up. Everybody gets to keep their "session" fee, of say $300, but only one is chosen to actually be used on the campaign with usage fees of usually thousands of dollars.

So if you're on your own, it's usually better, for small and medium sized jobs, to offer your fees as a full buy out for the media agreed on, including both "session" and "usage". For the huge ones, your hand will be held by an agent anyway.

To be honest, it is unusual for a radio and TV campaign to run more than a year and clients prefer to know that a "buy-out" means just that, with no surprise charges down the line.

When I give a quote, I always cut and paste (or use a key combination using Autotext software - **https://www.jitbit.com/autotext/** - really very useful!) the following list of things that the fee includes, and adapt the detail accordingly.

So I'd say something like:

"My fee includes:
Recording and professional studio time
Unlimited re-recordings if required
Audio editing and optimisation
Fast turnaround - usually same day
Supply as 24-bit wav or aiff master files
Full rights in all non-broadcast media for ever
30 days to pay via PayPal or bank transfer"

Note that the word "broadcast" in this list depends who you are sending this to; it could be a small company or end-client or a huge brand, as discussed before.

Once you have your own rate list, it is usually only a guide, not just for the size of client, but because sometimes a client is working on a lower budget project.

Once you have relationship with a regular client, and they ask you to do you a favour to record a script for $100 when it should be $200, what would you do? If they have been happy to pay you the full fee before, do you have any reason to disbelieve them about this new low-rate issue?

After all, the client may have a new end-client themselves, and they want to create a demo animation or video project to show what they can provide for them. If this is explained to you, you might even want to do it for free, but certainly a low rate would be the best compromise in this situation. After all, that new end client may love your voice so much when they sign up to your direct client, the production company, you will get much more work. In this sort of situation, it's an extension of providing a free custom demo, which you should be doing anyway.

If you're contacted by a brand-new client, who has just found your contact details, I usually say "what is your budget for the voiceover?" You may be well surprised, that the figure they give you, is greater than what was in your own fee guide. There is nothing wrong with not mentioning that you have a fee guide that they may not have seen. If, afterwards, they see your fee guide, don't feel that they are going to be angry towards you, thinking you have ripped them off or something!

There is usually something unusual in every job which you could claim that you needed to charge extra for, so that's why you didn't pipe up about the difference in the fee. It could be that there were unusual words to look up, there was extra editing involved, or that you had to drop another job to record that particular one first. Don't worry about it. It's not the client's own personal money most of the time; if $1000 was in the budget for the job, session and use, yet your Rate Card determined $600, just trouser the extra cash.

When it comes to putting together a quote for any client, as well as looking at the script, where you can immediately see how complex it is to record, both in terms of unusual words, and in the style of writing, you also need to find out if the client needs one file for the whole script, or individual files for each sentence or section as is normally needed by e-learning companies, or game companies, as this will take you much more time, even if you use clever automatic file splitting software like the excellent one in NCH Wavepad.

By the way, don't miss this trick when you are giving a quote. If it looks like the script is not going to be a one-off, and there could be future scripts, find out more details if your client has them. If you could offer a lower rate over a longer time period, everybody benefits. You'll get regular work, and the client will get a lower rate per script. So check this out if it's obvious it could be one of a series.

So what do you do for radio and TV commercials? For non-broadcast work, as I've mentioned, things are pretty straightforward. Every quote will be different, because every client is different. You may get an established advertising agency who know all the agreed rates from unions on "TVRs" and so on, and will simply give you a fee which I am sure you would be very happy with.

Then there are the agencies who haven't worked much with voice-overs, and if you sense this, you could simply send a link to one of the rate guides online to give them an idea of what sort of fee they should be paying.

They don't need to know, that you won't have any time or ability to check whether the commercial is still running after the agreed time, and I've got quite a few good deals out of simply sending clients not experienced with TV or radio commercial works to an established national or international rate card so they know the sort of fees they should be paying.

And finally, there are the low-budget production companies, where your voice could end up on a local radio or regional TV station anywhere around the world, and you would just have to agree or not agree with whatever is in their voice-over budget as you simply won't have the time to find out more.

The whole issue of quotes and fees, can be a minefield, and in this area, it's the only time when I sometimes wished I had an exclusive voice-over agent to deal with all this for me! But it's the only time. Most of the time, I am fully happy being a fully independent voiceover artist.

Now, I bet the real reason you are reading this chapter is you are wanting to see how much you can earn as a voice over artist. I am British, and in our culture it's pretty rude to ask someone how much they earn. However, apparently in Germany, I have been told, it is quite common to inquire about the salary of someone. It's just like asking someone in the street simply what the time is, or the quickest way to get to the Rathaus.

If you're really interested in my voiceover income, it has been over $100,000 a year for over 15 years now, and it goes up every year as more and more people find me and more regular work comes in; I should hit $200,000 in the year of writing due to the huge upsurge in online media work due to the global pandemic. Our media profession has been one of the lucky ones. I continue to keep up my marketing of course to make up for people who change talents as the direction of a campaign alters, or clients change their jobs completely or companies close down.

The thing is with our work, small things add up to big amounts. Just "do the math". If you do 5 small $50 jobs a day, that's $250 a day. If there are about 260 working days in a year, that's 260 x 250 = $65,000 to start with, and you will get jobs in the weekend as well, we all do. Then, say you get a long-term job every month like an audiobook or huge eLearning job that pays, say $2,000, and one big high paying job a month for a TV advert for another $2,000, and that is another 12 x 2 + 12 x 2 = 48k so that added to the 65 takes you into 6 figure territory.

Yes, of course you get taxed on the income, but once your equipment has been paid for, the only outgoings are power, internet, subscriptions and extra expenses. The only "problem" if you want to call it that is scaling your business more, as there is only one "you"; but you may want to start a little voice agency of your own and include "you" in the mix if you wish.

8
SETTING UP YOUR HOME STUDIO

If you've already set yourself up as a voiceover with your own home studio, and you're very happy with it, you can skip this section, and I've just put this in for newcomers to our industry, who might like to know my own recommendations.

First of all, <u>where</u> are you going to record? If you want to deliver "studio quality" recordings, you don't want any sounds in the background of course. No traffic noise or kids playing outside, no aeroplanes, no annoying neighbour with their leaf blower, but also, and many don't think about this, no low-level mains hum from wires, or whirring computer fans or hard disks even.

You can read your scripts off a silent device like a tablet, fan-less laptop or a monitor connected to a computer placed in a soundproofed vented box. No matter what, it's got to be silent in there! It's a really hard job to get rid of sound, and if you don't really know what you're doing, you may need to outsource this job to someone who specialises in acoustic solutions.

By the way, you may not want to set up your recording studio at home, but to hire some office space, and do it all there. Just make sure that your landlord will allow you to put up acoustic treatment and so on, just a word of warning before you start knocking things out! Be also aware that it is so convenient to "pop into" your home studio for a quick demo or a low-cost quick job after dinner and before pudding or whatever, that if you had to drive a few miles, you may not bother. Also I've had sessions with New Zealand starting at 4am UK time or going on until 2am in California, so you need to be sure you can access any commercial property you hire at all times, even weekends and public holidays.

It's not just getting rid of sound, you also have to treat the area where you're doing your recording, so it sounds acoustically "dead". It's easy to add reverberation, or echo, to any sound afterwards in post-production, but it is extremely hard, if not impossible, to get rid of it afterwards, no matter how clever your software is, and your client will usually want audio files without any coloration at all.

So clap your hands in the area you want to use to record in, and if you hear no reverberation at all, you've done a great job. If you do hear reverberation, then you need to surround yourself with sound absorbing surfaces. Your desk would have a blanket or a stiff foam pad on it and your walls might have acoustic blankets or even old duvets hung on them, you need anything that can absorb sound. The idea is not to have any shiny reflective surfaces, which can create these nasty reverberations.

It's OK to have a computer monitor directly behind the microphone, so you can read your scripts, but everything else needs to be soft! If you have a bit of cash when you are starting out, I would invest in professional acoustic tiles, or heavy acoustic blankets, but their placement is really determined by the space that you are in.

Now of course, if you are a professional voice over in for the long haul, you really ought to look into getting your own voice booth. Unless you live in the middle of the countryside, without any aeroplanes going across your house, and your room is perfectly soundproofed from the rest of the household, a voice booth is really essential. You may get away without having one for shorter scripts, but as soon as you get into longer e-Learning or audiobook work, or when you get directed by top agencies live from LA, you don't want to keep on stopping and starting when you hear pans rattling in your kitchen or the bins being collected outside in the street.

The average price for a voice booth is about $5,000 to $7,000, but it all depends on the size you want, and the thickness of the walls. Many people think these things are completely sound-proofed boxes, but no booth, unless it's got ridiculously thick walls filled with sand and a floating floor on mercury – and actually top radio stations have studios like these, I've worked in them for years - will ever stop all sound from getting in, but these booths will reduce it heavily, and with the acoustic tiles inside, will be a great location for recording.

When you get a booth though, it's not the end of the story, you still have to "tune it", and you may need to put "bass traps" in, (things shoved in the corners, effectively) or the clever placement of acoustic tiles to stop it sounding boxy, especially if it's quite a small booth.

Voice booths are extremely heavy, so if you are looking for one, check out the local companies wherever you live first, because the delivery costs can be very expensive and you will need help from fit people to construct it from all the heavy parts that will be left on your drive!

I live in northern England, and my voice booth happens to be a Kube one built in Yorkshire. But if you want a bit of flexibility, you might want to check out a company called Studio Bricks, who have got a system where you can put your voice booth together in manageable acoustic panels. This makes it quite easy to put together, without having to lift very heavy wall sections, and it means you can take it apart to move to another part of the house if you want to do, or even to a new home.

One tip about voice booths, if you have the room, go for one a bit bigger than the smallest you can find. Small booths can be a right pain to tune the "boxyness" out and they can get very stuffy in there. Yes, you can get air pumps to help ventilate voice booths, but they are never perfectly silent, no matter what the salesperson tells you. You need the flexibility to both sit down AND to stand up in your booth, and mine has two screens at both eye-levels, duplicating the computer output. The computer is a very quiet solid state one outside the booth.

What needs to be inside your voice booth? Ideally you would have bought one with a shelf inside, and some people just have a microphone in there with the USB interface box and a solid-state laptop which is completely silent, so there are no whirring fans or clicking hard drives to be picked up by the microphone. A solid-state fan-less laptop is really essential for us voice overs, especially when we are recording in hotel rooms for emergency scripts and so on, and we are very lucky to have technology like this at our fingertips.

But of course, where are you going to do your editing? You really don't want to edit on a tiny poor-quality loudspeaker that's inside a small laptop do you? Even quality headphones are not a good choice, and after recording, do you really want to keep the darn things on your head? To really listen to the quality of the sound, and any extraneous noises or hums or buzzes, you need monitors, studio loudspeakers. Your client will no doubt be listening on enormous quality studio speakers and will be very annoyed if they hear imperfections like lip smacks or low-level hum that you didn't pick up on!

So, after your recording in your booth, you will want to take your file from your laptop and do all your editing in a separate area with decent loudspeakers. What I do, is to have two completely different working areas. However I've actually got a mini studio built into my voice booth. In other words, on my shelf in the booth, I have the USB interface box with headphones, a keyboard, a computer monitor and a mouse and the actual computer is outside the voice booth connected by a load of cables. I have a mixer in the booth as well which is just for monitoring, and there are two shielded JBL loudspeakers connected to the wall. They are NOT powered or "active" loudspeakers that could create hum or buzz; the actual power amplifier is OUTSIDE the voice booth, but I can control the volume on the audio mixer in front of me. So I can record, and edit in there if I want to, saving a lot of time.

So, what equipment do you need to set up your own studio? Yes, you need a microphone, ideally a large diaphragm condenser microphone with an XLR connector. I have Neumann U87 and TLM103 microphones, but you don't need to splash out of high-end mikes like this at first. Inexpensive USB microphones can be perfectly OK for podcasting work, or lower end voice over work like basic eLearning, but when you get into the world of fussy audio production companies and advertising agencies recording you in your home studio, they will want to know that you have a pretty high specification microphone, and these would NOT be USB mikes. They would be large diaphragm condenser mikes with "XLR" connectors.

I don't know if this would ever come up in a pub quiz, but the "XLR" name comes from the three connectors, X for Earth, L for Left channel, and R for Right channel, and of course us voiceovers have only one mouth so our microphones are actually MONO!

The thing is that USB microphones are not just usually found at the lower end of the price range, but they are also not flexible. You CAN plug them straight into your computer, that's really convenient, BUT you can't plug a USB microphone into a mixer, a podcaster machine like, say, the Rode Podcaster or one of the Zoom models, or a solid-state audio recorder.

All mikes should be used with an adjustable arm mount, never with a holder that is placed on your desk that can pick up your table rumble. Buy the best you can afford, and one that takes the weight of your microphone and holds still at sitting AND standing level.

Your microphone needs to go into a shock mount as well. This is a suspension device that prevents a mic from picking up further rumbling sounds. It's mounted on the end of a microphone stand and holds the mic. Special rubber bands absorb unwanted vibrations. The type of shock mount totally depends on the particular microphone and sometimes shock mounts are bundled with the mike. If a shock mount is not bundled with the microphone you buy, there are plenty of 3rd party ones if you look on Amazon, but make sure that the mount will actually fit your microphone. You need to measure the diameter of your mike and make sure that the shock mount will not just fit it but accept its weight as well.

When using sensitive microphones, it's essential to avoid the plosives and sibilant sounds that may be picked up by the mic. That's exactly the job for a "pop filter" – it's a compact screen that connects to a microphone stand with a clamp. You can position the filter right in front of the microphone capsule and it will help diffuse the air generated by the notorious plosive P's and T's. Depending on the model, the screen can be metallic or made of a nylon fabric. I recommend double pop filters, they're excellent; they also help to protect the condenser capsule from tiny particles of saliva that inevitably fly out when you speak. Over time, contact with moisture will corrupt the sensitive capsule. You need to wash the pop filter at least once a month for hygiene purposes. Spray both sides with antibacterial fluid, and then pour boiling water on it and then pat dry carefully with paper towels.

If you have an XLR analogue microphone, you also need a USB interface box which can convert the analogue audio signal into digital that the computer can understand. There are many types of USB interface boxes but the Steinberg UR22 and any of the Focusrite range are particularly good for professional use. They have an input control, and usually a decent quality headphone amplifier as well so you would monitor things via this box by plugging your headphones into it. You wouldn't monitor from your actual computer.

When you wire up your microphone into your USB interface box, and then connect this into your computer, you then need to make this box the default audio for your whole computer, and also for any audio software you're using. Just ignore the computer's internal sound card.

With a microphone that has an analogue XLR socket, it can be connected into a digital audio recorder, and / or into a USB interface, which connects everything to the computer. My system is "belts and braces", in other words, I have a back-up system. The output from my microphone goes into the USB interface that's connected to the computer and also, via a "Y" lead adaptor into an audio solid state recorder. So, when I record anything, I actually record using the software on my computer, and also I put the solid state recorder into record mode as well.

There are two reasons for doing this. First of all the computer could glitch, and I have had problems with the driver for the USB interface creating annoying dropouts, so your solid-state recorder is a backup recording that shouldn't have any of these problems on.

The second thing is that the solid-state recorder has its input record level slightly lower than that of the computer. If a script has a particularly loud or shouty moment, if it is distorted on the computer version, it shouldn't be distorted on the solid-state recorder backup version. This system has been used by me for years, and I do recommend that you follow this as well, because it would be awful to record particularly long scripts or "that perfect take" and find that there are glitch issues or nothing has been recorded at all.

You can either use Mac or Windows operating systems, it's up to you. Most audio editing software is available for both. If you're really serious about this career, you need Adobe Audition via Adobe's Creative Cloud, and to subscribe to that. It has so many excellent features, is very robust, and the shortcuts that it can offer you, where you push a single key on your keyboard, which can do multiple things, is worth the time saved alone. Maybe you won't need more than Audition, but I also have Adobe Premiere Pro and After Effects, the video programs, for jobs where my voiceover needs to be synchronised with another video with another language on.

I like Adobe's Acrobat for far better control over reading and stripping out text in pdf scripts, and an Adobe subscription gives you access to everything. If you really can't afford Adobe software, I can recommend the free Audacity program or NCH's wonderful Wavepad, which has a file cutting feature I use all the time for e-Learning projects when I'm asked to cut my long recording into many separate files!

So you've got your microphone, your interface with the computer, and a very quiet area that is acoustically treated. What else do you need? You will need a comfortable pair of headphones so that you can be directed on those sessions. When you are directed, by a client in a remote location, you mustn't have the loudspeakers in your studio or booth on.

You would normally click a button on your USB interface box, turn the loudspeakers down or off, and put your headphones on. This prevents any comments or noise or buzz from your client getting into your clean recordings. My headphones are Beyerdynamic DT250's that offer great clear sound and are soft and very comfortable to wear. I have gone through about 6 pairs of these as I keep wearing them out!

You'll also need some sort of loudspeaker monitoring, and I personally like quality powered speakers and a small mixer by the side of me, I have an eight-channel mixer just for monitoring, and you may not need this to start with, somehow you've got to be able to listen back on loudspeakers as you do not want to be wearing headphones all day, as it will give you a headache, and will drive you mad!

You need to be connected to the Internet of course, and you need an Internet speed of at least 20 Mb/sec download and upload 10 Mb per second. It is possible to work on Wi-Fi, but to be honest, if your studio computer can be connected by wire rather than Wi-Fi, to your router, then do it. It will be much more stable and usually faster as well.

Other technical expenses in your world of being a professional voiceover will come from subscriptions to other various things. As well as the obvious subscription to Microsoft for using Word, Excel and PowerPoint, plus their email program, Outlook, I subscribe to WeTransfer, the system to send big files, such as your large 24 bit wav audio files via a link you can send in email. You can get away with the free service, but it's much more professional to have your own WeTransfer channel where you can put your logo up and marketing pictures and information about your services that the client can see when they are downloading your files. You get far bigger amounts of data use as well as a WeTransfer channel subscriber. It's a great service, very reliable, and when clients get a secure link they feel more secure than if they got a link to Dropbox or Google Docs where they may not be sure who else has access to their precious files.

So here is my list of recommended gear to buy for a professional voiceover set-up. Don't forget to keep your receipts for all the equipment and your accountant will be able to offset the purchases against tax for you.

RECOMMENDED EQUIPMENT FOR A PROFESSIONAL HOME VOICEOVER STUDIO

SOLID STATE FAN-LESS LAPTOP
SECOND MONITOR FOR STANDING DELIVERY
VESA MOUNT FOR SECOND MONITOR
MICROPHONE
MICROPHONE CRADLE
POP FILTER
MICROPHONE STAND
CABLES
USB INTERFACE BOX
HEADPHONES
POWERED MONITORS (LOUDSPEAKERS)
POWER AMPLIFIER (If required)
SOLID STATE AUDIO RECORDER
AUDIO EDITING SOFTWARE
ACOUSTIC CURTAINS
ACOUSTIC TILES

Some notes about the gear:

SOLID STATE FANLESS LAPTOP You don't need to have a highly powerful computer to read the scripts off and for audio editing after editing. That's good, because the more power the computer has, the more likely it will have pesky whirring fans to cool down the hard-working CPU and that sound will be picked up by your sensitive microphone. You need a laptop with a completely solid-state drive or drives, that is with no clicking old fashioned Hard Disks, but also no fans for CPU cooling. I repeat, your laptop must have NO FANS! These machines do exist (and cool by using heat distributing paste and so on) but quite often computer salespeople and even the websites of manufacturers are wrong in saying their machines do not have fans, when in fact they do, and they kick in when overheating. These people don't realise how important it is for us voice artists to have a completely silent machine.

You need machines that are powerful enough to do the recording and editing, but not so powerful that it will need whirring fans to cool the CPU; using instead thermal glues and heat sinks, which are of course silent. You could read the scripts off a silent tablet or even paper, and edit on another computer afterwards, but assuming you need an all-in-one laptop solution, these are our recommended choices below at the time of writing. Models change all the time, so just check that your choice is completely fan-less.

By the way, if you need to do video editing as well as audio editing, a very powerful computer, then a small laptop won't do. You will probably need a tower computer which WILL have fans. Here you'll need a powerful beast with about 3GHz speed, 64GB of RAM and a rack of 5TB hard drives to store the large HD or 4K video files. So, you'll need to hide your whirring, clattering tower computer some metres away, maybe in a ventilated sound proofed cupboard and connect everything to your booth via long active USB cables.

SECOND MONITOR FOR STANDING DELIVERY

Have you noticed that you give a different type of voiceover performance when you're standing and when you're sitting?

Certainly to stand rather than sitting is better for dynamic acting roles; have you ever tried to be furiously angry sitting down?! Your breathing is better standing, and you often need to take less breaths. It's better for your long-term care of your back too.

In your recording location, you could read your scripts on your desk where you are sat, but have a higher shelf at eye-level when you wish to record standing up and move the laptop up there. But that means moving all the pesky wiring as well. It's not essential, but many voiceovers like myself have a second monitor screwed to the wall at standing eye level. All modern computers have 2 video outputs. Just check what the output socket is on the computer and the input socket of the second monitor.

These sockets could be DP (Display Port) MiniDP (Mini Display Port), HDMI (High Definition Multimedia Interface) or mini HDMI! It can get confusing but check before you order. Note that these second monitors need power and that is often these days via a separate USB-C cable, so you'll need this as well to plug into a USB power source, either your laptop or a main USB source.

IMPORTANT: When you connect the second monitor up, the computer may think that you want to use it as a "playback" audio device as default. So if your audio playback doesn't work after connecting up another monitor, go back into SETTINGS and ensure that both INPUT and OUTPUT default audio is set to your USB interface, like the Focusrite or Steinberg box.
By the way, the second monitor is much more useful when it's the same aspect ratio as your main one. Most laptops are 16:9 aspect ratio, the same as our HD home TV screens. Your second monitor will be much more useful when it's the same aspect ratio.

Once you have the second monitor connected, you'd right click on the desktop, click Display Options and then choose "Extend" monitor is you'd like, for example, the script displayed on the top one, and Adobe Audition running on the bottom one, or "Duplicate" if you would rather have the same on both.

Note that to connect it to a universal "VESA" mount to attach to a wall, make sure the monitor has this feature as not all don't. If not, you'll have to prop it on a shelf!

VESA MOUNT FOR SECOND MONITOR

The four holes on the back of your second monitor will be compatible with the VESA system. (Video Electronics Standards Association) Thank goodness all the manufacturers spoke to each other to standardise this! Your big HD/4K TV at home will probably have the "big" VESA version, but these small monitors will have one of the "small" VESA versions. VESA comes in 50, 75 and 100mm versions. Check your monitor's screw holes!

All mounts you buy should have holes for all options. One word of caution, sometimes the mount often comes with various sets of screws to connect the mount to the monitor. Don't use the big screws on your small LED monitor as you could easily screw into the screen itself and ruin it.

MICROPHONE

It's so important to get the best microphone that you can afford, and you may find a great second-hand bargain from a closing down recording studio; just make sure it hasn't been dropped or screamed at by countless rock singers! Avoid "USB" microphones. It may seem really convenient to be able to plug a microphone straight into a computer for the computer to "read it", but usually the quality of USB microphones isn't that great for professional voice work, and you will definitely find that it is not flexible. For example, you can't plug a USB microphone into an audio mixer, or into a solid-state recorder. For voiceover work you need microphones that are analogue large capacitor microphones, (not "dynamic") which will need an analogue-to-digital converter box, but these are not hugely expensive and will give you a decent headphone amplifier built in.

MICROPHONE CRADLE

There are loads of suitable decent large diaphragm microphones out there suitable for voice over work, however you may get just the microphone without a cradle. A cradle is a mount that sensitively holds the microphone with various rubber or springy cords that ensure that vibrations don't get through to the microphone itself. It is really important to have this. You will be surprised how rumbles from the floor or just you touching the desktop can get through to the microphone.

Very important: Make sure the mount you order fits your mike and measure the diameter of your microphone body before you order. Also determine the size of the screw that will connect it to the mike stand too, there are many different sizes!

POP FILTER

Some shock mounts have a built in pop-filter but usually they are not that great. For close-up work, you need to have a very good quality filter to stop the nasty "plosive" sounds from getting the microphone on "p" sounds in particular. Double ones are very good, and they don't have to be huge in diameter. In fact a little one of about 3-4 inches across is better as you can see clearly the exact centre of the microphone capsule which is where you should be speaking to get he maximum resonance from your mouth.

MICROPHONE STAND

Do not buy a microphone stand that sits on the desktop, especially if you haven't got a decent cradle. You need a boom-arm type or one on a spring arm like the old "Anglepoise" lamps. These make it easy to yank into position whether you are sitting or standing and it should just stay there. The ideal "average" voiceover position is 4 inches from the pop filter, which is again 3-4 inches away from the centre of the microphone capsule.

CABLES

What's the point of buying a top specification microphones and then connect it to your USB interface box with a cheap cable? The cable should be as short as it can be, and screened, so that it doesn't pick up any hum from around the house. Also go for gold contacts. Don't sink a ship for a halfpenny of tar, as old sailors used to say!

USB INTERFACE BOX

If you haven't a USB microphone which I highly recommend that you don't, you need one of these USB interface boxes to convert the analogue audio signals from your condenser microphone into digital ones that you can record and edit. They also provide the +48 Volts needed to power the condenser microphone.

These devices have an input control, so you can get the audio level right on your audio software input, and a switch so you can "direct monitor" yourself, rather than just listen on playback. You'll need this switch on remote directed voiceover sessions.

The headphone jack is very useful especially if your mixer or powered speakers don't have this facility. Remember when you set this up, the USB interface box will take control of ALL your computer audio, so you won't be usually be able to use the headphone socket on your laptop or computer.

If you are doing podcast recording with a co-presenter, you'll need a dual channel device, not a "Solo" one. In other words each of your microphones would go into a separate XLR input, and there will be two lots of controls, but with a single USB input to the computer.

HEADPHONES

Though many voice actors don't bother to wear headphones for most of the time, you will find it useful if you're a bit tired, or having difficulty focusing on the script. Hearing your voice loud in your ears can really help! Of course you'll have to wear the "cans" when you're being directed by a remote client on one of the internet systems around. You can't have any speakers on. In-ear buds are no good, nor the headphones that are placed on your ear, as sound will bleed through to your mike. So they have to be headphones that cover the ears completely.

POWERED MONITORS When you are editing your voiceover recordings, don't use headphones or the tiny horrible loudspeaker you get in your laptop. Connect the output from the USB audio interface (For example the Focusrite) and connect it to a pair of powered speakers. Yes, I know our voices are mono, and we only have one mouth, but it's just nicer to hear stuff on two speakers, isn't it? Powered speakers save the hassle of getting a separate amplifier and all the wiring, BUT they have to be very good quality or else they may well create hum or hiss even when no signal is being put through them.

SOLID STATE AUDIO RECORDER You may wish to just record on a solid-state recorder, and transfer to a computer for editing, or use it as a backup, so you'd record **both** on the computer and the recorder using a "Y-Lead" from the microphone.

Whatever one you choose has to have XLR inputs and 48 volt Phantom power capability to drive the condenser microphone. Most of these are now made for musicians so that's why many are 4 or 8 track, we of course, only need one channel.

9
TYPICAL "ROOKIE" MISTAKES

As well as being a professional voice over myself, I have also directed very many recording sessions using other voice over artists in my own studio and in countless radio stations and commercial production studios, some experienced and some not so, as well as training many. Here is my not exhaustive list of issues that people new to the voiceover industry do which they soon learn to get out of, if they want to survive! I hope you'll find this useful.

THE WEBSITE THAT DOESN'T SELL THEM OR THEIR STRENGTHS

Someone starting out often fills their website just with showreels of mock adverts for radio or TV, selling brands that would in real life simply not be suitable for their voice, sex or age, and using scripts with a voice style for real big-name brands which just would not suit their corporate image anyway. Big mistake. It's also crazy just having commercial showreels - as you'll see in the "50 Voiceover" jobs section in the appendix, commercials are only a small part of what a voiceover can offer. In fact at the time of writing, I personally haven't recorded a radio or TV ad for about 3 weeks now, yet I've never been busier recording really well-paid corporate films, documentaries, museum and escape room character voices and so on, and unless you get network radio or TV jobs, the pay for local and even regional ads can be very poor indeed.

THE LATE ROOKIE

There is nothing worse being in a recording studio with the client, and ad agency people, trying to make small talk with the clock ticking, and the voice over artist has not arrived yet. And then when they do, there's always some lame excuse like not finding a parking meter or something. They soon learn that if you turn up about 15 minutes early, there's a chance to chat with other staff, get to know them, and maybe get some extra work booked in while you are there. It also gets your breath back, and an opportunity to relax, have a drink and read through the script.

NOISES OFF

They wear clothes that rustle terribly or have bangles or jewellery that rattle around as they speak. They then take offence when they're asked to take the stuff off. And surely, they HAVE switched off their phone haven't they? Surely?

STAND BACK – THERE'S NOTHING TO SEE!

They want to get too close to the microphone; even though you have carefully positioned the microphone and pop filter, and taken a good sound level, they insist on leaning forward like they're talking to someone in a noisy bar who can't hear them.

NOT PREPARED

The rookie VO arrives at the session having not read the brief, seen the script or even thought about the job, expecting a nice cup of tea and a bun and a briefing meeting before recording, when most times, every second counts to get the darn thing on air

MIND THE GAP

When the script hasn't been read through, or understood, quite often the rookie voice over leaves long gaps between each sentence, which means extra time for the engineer having to edit them out, but more importantly, when the client is listening on the loudspeakers in the control room, they can't get a full sense of timing or the flow of the whole piece.

THIRD HEAD NOT WORKING

Sometimes the rookie voice over says words completely wrong. No, we're not recording Sheridan's "The Rivals", and you don't have Mrs Malaprop in the booth do you? Quite often I have stopped the recording, to say "you have said that word wrongly", and I've not been believed, unless I played it back to them! So obviously their "third head" monitoring technique hasn't been developed yet. More on this later.

TAKE, NOT GIVE DIRECTION

I have worked with various arrogant voice actors, who seemed to think they knew how the script should be performed better than the client sat in the studio. As we all should know, this is not a good idea. The number one rule in much of business is that "the client is always right" - yes, even if they are wrong! If you are asked for your opinion, obviously give it, but make sure you are not stepping on any toes, or embarrassing the advertising agency who have no doubt given their own steer on the feel of the performance to the end client.

TIME IS MONEY

Just because this session is the only thing in the rookie voice overs diary, doesn't mean that everyone else on the session have got such an easy day! Make a small amount of small talk, but don't hold court with long irrelevant anecdotes that just eat up and waste valuable session time!

10
WARM-UPS AND VOICE TRAINING

Wasn't it Abraham Lincoln who said **"Give me an hour to cut down a tree, and I'll spend the first 59 minutes sharpening the axe?"** You shouldn't just get out of bed, lurch into the booth, grab a script, and read it. Even though the client says it's URGENT and you MUST record it right away...there's the old adage, less haste more speed. So, while you're doing some of the warm-ups, I'm about to share with you, you can multitask as well. Read the instructions the client has sent, and listen to the previous version maybe which has a voice style they need and check pronunciations and so on. Preparation is so key to this type of work; you don't want to trip up on words or waste your time recording something that has to be done again when the deadline is even nearer than last time, do you?

You should really warm up your voice before you start using your voice, particularly if you're doing a hard sell or shouty stuff, or else you're going to really strain your voice. The first thing you do basically is to "take your mouth to the gym". Now, most of us are lazy. Most of us don't like to open our mouths. And so we just sort of slur our way through the day.

Obviously, we voiceovers can't do that. But you may find that your brain wants you to say words clearly, but they don't actually come out clearly. Why is that? Maybe it's because the muscles around your mouth haven't had a workout recently.

So here's a good exercise. It's my "QEQR" exercise. You have to be prepared to really exaggerate and lose your inhibitions.

So if you wouldn't mind doing a Q sound now, please for me. "Q".... Off you go...

And then you go "E" ... stretch your mouth ....E

...and then you go. "Q" again and then "R".

R really opens the mouth that so you simply repeat the letters. Q E Q R. You may look strange, but one of the characteristics of being a voice over is that you don't mind making a fool of yourself.

Hopefully, you're tingling a little bit around the mouth. And that's because basically you've given your mouth a good stretch. You're using muscles which you don't normally use... you're stretching, just like you stretch your whole body in the morning before you get up and make your breakfast. So here you are, stretching the muscles around the mouth gently by doing QEQR. And if you do that 10 times before you start to voice over, you will notice yourself speaking so much clearer and you'll be pronouncing the ends of words better.

The second exercise I'll mention is basically a humming exercise, a real deep hum and just hum for as low as you can. It's good for meditation and relaxation too.

Try and get some resonance in your mouth when you hum as well. Let's sort of chew it around and so you sort of feel your chest vibrate. Very important to get your chest vibrate. No matter what kind of voice you've got and whether you're a male or a female.

Humming is great. It really is. And if you're on a long journey in the car, you can do sort of 10 minutes at a time. And no one can tell you're making a fool of yourself, but you'll notice your voice get more resonant and deep if you wanted to get deep as well. But just gives you some extra semitones at the bottom of the scale in there, which really helps a lot.

Thirdly, I'd like you to yawn and raise your eyebrows too. At the start of a yawn, you'll notice how it's not just the mouth that opens, and your larynx goes down, but also a little bit, the soft palate goes UP. Inside your mouth, at the top near the teeth there is the HARD PALATE. Go further back and this becomes the SOFT PALATE. So in this exercise you are feeling for this and raising this soft palate as you do this BIG YAWN.

This will help your voice become more flexible to create nice big sounding notes and sound less nasal. As raising the soft palate cuts off the voice from going through the nose.

In fact here's a test you can do now. Hum the word HANG, and hold the nose. See...the note is coming out of the nose, because as you pinch the nose, the sound is reduced. So now hum AAAH. You have now raised the soft palate, so when you pinch the nose, you still hear the note! You have now reduced nasality!

I must mention that the start of the yawn can give you some wonderful variations on voices if you're into character work. Try half yawning, holding it there without getting too tense and start speaking. Can you create a variety of different character voices that you couldn't before?

Anyway, those are the main Warm-Up exercises I'll mention, apart from going into the bathroom and getting some water, especially if you're just out of bed in the morning and gargle or gargle for about 10, 15 seconds. Spit it out. Use more clean water, and gargle for another 10, 15 seconds. Some people like lemon juice as well. That might perk you up. Some people say don't drink any milk at all, it doesn't affect me personally, but other professional voice users have said that it increases the mucus levels. That's a very basic list of warm-ups but you may have your own favourites you'd like to try. I do my own warm-ups before the morning and the afternoon recording sessions.

I have put together many video-based training courses on voice training including a 30-day plan and one for specifically creating resonance and depth in a voice. If you'd like to find out more, please visit www.VoiceoverMasterclass.com

11
THINKING OF THE LISTENER

It's essential to keep in mind the typical or ideal listener to whatever type of script you're recording. You need to think of just one person, not a group. This is something that was drummed into me when I first started in radio presentation many years ago; any form of pluralism was banned.

A radio host, even though he or she knew that thousands of people may be listening at that moment, would always refer to people in the singular, never the plural. So it would be never be *"It looks like rain so, folks, take your umbrellas today!"* You would say, (if you really had to say such a naff line on the radio) *"It looks like rain, don't forget to take your umbrella today."*

Even if people are listening or even watching television in a group, listeners and viewers still like to be referred to in the singular. What works in broadcasting also works for the voiceover world as well, especially when the output is audiobooks or podcasts, which is even more of an intimate experience.

Try and imagine the type of person who is listening, whatever type of script it is. In fact, you can try to create the "ideal listener" and you can image where they are listening to your voice and what's sort the mood they're in. Are they going to be fully receptive to learn, or do they need to be persuaded to buy something? This may sound a bit unnecessary, but, honestly, it will really help you to focus your mind and to give a consistent performance for that type of script.

Imagine the person's face, maybe someone you know, listening to an ad on the radio or on their phone, or for an audiobook, in their car on a long journey, on a train, or maybe they are lying in bed at night listening to another chapter of your voice. This is an absolutely essential technique to really relate to the listener.

Think of a potential customer if you're recording a corporate promo or an advert. You're not just the "announcer", you really need to BELIEVE that you have put years of work and maybe your life savings into this particular venture and you are now selling it to the world.

Maybe you're recording a factual book about meditation techniques; it can be incredibly helpful to think of an "ideal listener" and simply read for them, and this helps you sound "in tune" with the information even if you are sight-reading and you're not an expert on the subject. So you may want to read this book to a "25 year old psychology graduate who is about to embark on further studies in meditation"...or " a 40 year old divorcee who is trying to turn her life around after years of abuse from an unfaithful husband".... Or whatever! This isn't crazy new-age stuff, this technique really helps to focus the voice style and to lock it there. You're not just reading words off a script!

If a friend of yours is a fan of the author whose novel you are reading as an audiobook, read "just for them", and you'll never believe how much extra power this gives to your longevity in the booth and by thinking this way, it's amazing how suddenly you naturally "get" what the book is about, the tone, the pace, the passion, it all comes together, you aren't simply just "reading".

For live venue announcements, like at theme parks and rail stations, you also have to keep in your head the listener, but not due to their personalities, but for practical acoustic reasons. Years ago I regularly presented the pre-match entertainment for Manchester United at the Old Trafford stadium as part of my work for Piccadilly Radio. I had to make sure that my diction and projection was perfect and the speed of delivery compensated for the insane echo reflections around the ground, without speaking so slow it would sound like I was on Valium.

12
THE FIVE VOCAL ELEMENTS

When I have been training complete beginner voiceover artist and voice actors in the past, they have often told me that they found it useful for me to explain about the "five vocal elements" when receiving a new script to record. It's something you only really need to concentrate on when you start out, because this will become second nature to you after a while.

Once you've received a script and you've determined the target audience to pitch the level of understanding to and you've checked pronunciations, as well as punctuation, you also need to assign parameters to these five basic vocal elements.
And it's important to memorize these because when you're starting out, quite often you change one and then something else changes as well. And you shouldn't do that. They should be completely separate.

The elements are:
1 - Voice style   2 – Volume   3 – Tone and emotion   4 – Speed 5 – Pitch.

1 - Voice Style.
Are you a straight narrator? What type? Are you aiming at a consumer or is it an internal training script? Who is the ideal end-listener? What accent or character voice do they want you to use? Maybe it's a sound of a particular part of your showreel or demo that the client likes; if they haven't told you, ask them. They must have heard something from you for them to book you.   Like the way you said that advert for a particular client or whatever.

Ask them specifically for what they liked the sound of. Remember the client is always right – so if they say you need to voice like " in the section about the airport at 22 seconds in on your corporate showreel # 5", you'll know what they mean. So, capture that feel, accent and sound in your head and stick to it. That may be all you need to get started, but it's useful to break the preparation down into four further elements.

2 - Volume.
Now, in the old days, particularly in North America, radio and TV listeners had to endure being barked at by a loud announcer voice in adverts and voice overs in general. Now, that was partly because microphones were not as sensitive as they are today. Plus, whole families gathered round the radio or TV then. The announcer was addressing the crowd, so to speak, as if they were at a ball game.

Well, these days, of course, people consume media mostly on their own. Microphones are very sensitive. So does the client want a gentle, intimate read at a low volume, or would the read need to have more authority and a loud volume with more energy, the so called "Hard Sell" style?

3 - Tone and emotion.
Well, back to the old days of radio again. They used to have a "tone" control on it, which affected crudely the bass and treble equalisation. But in the world of voice overs, we really mean for "tone" the word "emotion".

 Often, I get people contact me who haven't got English as their first language and they say they want the read more "emotional", and when they say this I feel as if they want me to cry during it, but I know what they mean!

It's the emotion of the voice for a script. Think of the various moods and states you have, and you'd probably have a voice emotion to match it. Ecstatic, desperate, passionate, enthusiastic, sarcastic, unhappy, crazed, phased out, furious, concerned, stoic, depressed, perky and so on. So whatever adjective you can think of, there's a voice to go with it. It's very important to lock in, however, and stay on that one tone, on that one emotion and sustain it for the whole script.

4 – Speed.
What tempo does the script need to be? You know, sometimes you're given an over written script, with simply too many words for the tone and emotion that they want. If you have an obvious, soft toned script but over, say, 100 words to shoehorn into a 30 second commercial slot, it's going to sound too fast and the emotion will be lost, won't it?

Well, it's "words to the wise" time, isn't it? You need to discuss this tactfully with the client to have some less important words cut out. Generally, enthusiasm and excitement need a faster speed or pace than a script describing refinement or beauty. Just ask the client what they're looking for.

But remember, at the end of the day, the customer is always right and sometimes you have to do what they ask. They'll soon realise that you're right!   If you like, send them a demo showing it'll sound awful cramming too many words in. They'll understand it when they hear it!

5 – Pitch.

Now, you have to ask yourself questions like, would this script be more effective in a low register, a middle pitch or higher up as if you were tense or addressing a crowd?

If the client hasn't already told you, look at the words and determine what the script is meant to convey – think also of the target audience - and make a decision on finding an appropriate pitch.

Determining a pitch range is also essential here. If you're reading an audio book for little children, a pitch range that swoops wildly between very high and very low is often appropriate, isn't it, children? If you're recording a legal court report, an often monotone delivery is required as long as the correct words or sentence sections are emphasized correctly.

So these are the Five Vocal Elements.

Once you've identified each of those five elements for your script, if you're asked to adjust one of them, please be very careful that this does not affect another one.

For example, if you're reading a script that has these elements determined:
1 - Voice style - London Cockney working class
2 – Volume - loud
3 - Tone and emotion - sarcastic
4 - Speed, slow
5 - Pitch, mid.

So for this script they want me to be a London cockney working class and a bit sarcastic, bit slow. Okay. But the producer now can't fit all the words into the 30 second spot time, can he? So he's asked for a retake that is faster. The problem with that is that I'll go a bit faster and suddenly I find myself raising a pitch as well. That's no good is it? So change one. Don't change any other.

If you're a new voiceover and you've found all this a bit confusing, don't worry, after a while all this will become second nature to you. You'll open up a script and look at the clients needs and say to yourself, "Yes, it's "one of those", no problem!

13

THE "THIRD HEAD" TECHNIQUE OF SELF-MONITORING

All my tips and techniques in this book are directed at voiceover artists who are working in home studios, so I assume that you will normally be on your own. An incredibly important skill that you will need when you are recording material on your own, and if you aren't being directed by headphones from your client, is to be able to monitor yourself very well.

In other words, you've got to listen carefully to what you are saying at all times. This skill or technique is so important to get right, and it will save you making mistakes and sending off files with errors in that will only get thrown back at you by angry clients.

I call this technique the "third head" technique, and this is a homage to the old reel to reel tape recorder. Before the days of digital, ¼ inch magnetic tape used to be spooled from one side to another, going across three tape heads at 15 inches per second; or just 7.5 inches per second if you were a semi-pro, or on a budget!

The first tape head de-magnetised the tape as it went over it. It wiped it clean ready for recording. The second head recorded what you wanted to record on it by modulating the magnetic particles on the tape. The third head was a "play" head, and monitored what had been recorded on the tape.

So the "third head technique" is basically the human equivalent of this.

It's a way of monitoring yourself very carefully, so that if you make a mistake, you'll know straight away, and you would stop and pick up. I have to say that the third head technique is difficult to teach, some people either get it, or simply don't get it. The people who don't get it are the ones who play back the recording afterwards, and can't believe they messed up, because they didn't notice at the time!

It helps a lot of course, if you have someone else with you monitoring, you learn a lot from feedback on directed sessions online or in an external studio, but I know many of you will be recording material on your own. You would certainly be rehearsing on your own, so you need to learn this technique. To get into the third head mode, it's almost like developing an out of body experience, so you create another "you" that is just listening not speaking, while the real "you" carries on talking.

Another way to think about it, is that you earmark a part of your brain to just listen to yourself while the rest of your brain gets on with the narration. When you get really good at it, you'll be able to notice individual words that haven't been quite enunciated as best as they could be.

You cannot only train the brain to do this, but you can push it even harder to use a "look forward" technique as well by the way. So while your eyes are reading and your mouth is reading the words off the script, and your ears are monitoring, your eyes are ALSO looking ahead to the next line or even the next sentence.

That way, even though you would have rightly, studied the script before recording, you can prepare for some unusual words. I have to do this regularly for urgent news bulletins that need to be sight-read and have to be recorded fast pr done live on-air. I have to use my eye to look ahead when I'm sight reading so that I can prepare myself to say words the correct way, and this saves so much time stopping and picking up and editing out the mess afterwards.

14

MANAGING CLIENTS – ASKING FOR WHAT YOU NEED

Once you have got regular clients, it's easy to work with them because they know what you need, and you know what they need as well. For example, I have a client who sends me scripts in exactly the way I like laid out, with a decent pronunciation guide all on one mp3 file, with every word spoken three times at different speeds, and I know they always like the recording ready compressed as a 24 bit wav, and I know they will pay me very quickly. So that's fine, if it's someone you know. But when it's a brand-new client - all bets are off!

When you're contacted by a new potential client, you do get a good idea of how experienced they are working with voice overs. If they say something vague like "how do you work", or "do you write your own scripts" or something, then I know I have got someone who needs a little bit of handholding.

If I am busy, and I think maybe this enquiry from a potential new client could be a bit of a waste of time, I do have a piece of boilerplate, that I have in my trusty Autotext software as a pre-set, and I simply reply something like this:

Thank you very much for your interest in my voiceover services. Please send your script through to me and I would be pleased to record it in my broadcast quality studio. Please ensure the script is fully checked, and let me know please how to pronounce any unusual names or technical terms (such as acronyms, etc.) A link to a recording with any unusual names or other words being said would be appreciated if there are any words which may be unusual for me. Where is this recording to be used please?Then let me know the style of voiceover (corporate, casual, character voice etc.) and any timing or pace considerations.
All the best, Peter

You are welcome to use this and adapt it how you see fit. After you have sent this and maybe you have got some more details back, that is when you ask for their voiceover budget or give your quote for the job, once you have seen the actual script. At this point if you do have a time waster, they may either disappear completely, or ask for some kind of discount.

Here is a list of the information you need from the client in an ideal situation, I'm sure you'll be able to add a few more with your own experience!

- The script, as a Word document or Text, not a PDF that has to be converted to be edited to be marked up.
- Any unusual names and words that can't be found from HowjSay, Forvo or the usual sources to be highlighted with a link or to a pronunciation audio guide.
- A pronunciation guide as a single audio file, each word said 3 times – normal speed, very slowly (even syllable by syllable for some very hard words), and normal speed again.
- A link to see the video (If applicable) and maybe a placeholder voiceover, or at least the selected music so you can determine the mood of the voice.
- The accent required – BBC British, Kiwi, Scottish, GenAm, Mid-Atlantic, Bronx etc.
- A link to an existing showreel of a voice they like or a part of one of your own showreels.
- Then questions like: Where is this to be used?
- Who is the target audience?
- Will English be the first language of the ideal target audience?
- What is your budget or do I give you a quote?
- When do you need the recording by?
- Can I self-direct or do you want to direct via headphones?

- If so, what system do you want to use? (ipDTL, Zoom, Riverside etc.)
- What time is the directed session and in what time zone?
- Timing considerations? Does it have to fit a set duration? Does each paragraph need to sync with another version of the video?
- Do you need clear editing gaps in between each sentence?
- What is the output format? Usually the industry standard is -3dB Normalized waveforms, Mono, 24 bit, 48KHz sampling, .wav or .aiff files.
- Do you want every section as separate files or one big file? Do they have to be named in a certain way?
- What is the project number and / or Purchase Order number for the job?

A lot of questions here, but I hope that most of your clients will be media-savvy enough to understand what you need for each specific project and what they need back. If they don't understand why you need this information, you may have a "difficult client".

15
NATURAL VOICE ACTING

Have you ever been asked to deliver a scripts in a completely "natural" style, in other words like a "real person" in a "real situation"?

To underline and to emphasize this, quite often the accompanying brief of the voice over script or demo job says "Please - no announcer voice!"

This "announcer" term comes from radio sports announcers in the mid-20th century, who, particularly in America, developed a type of high octane, high-energy, very fast method of speaking, that was adapted into many TV and radio commercials, where the advertiser wanted to get most bang for their buck.

So when your brief says "natural", or "not announcer", this basically means they want you to sound like the man or woman in the street, and not like in the affected style of a voiceover artist. This means that you need to deliver the script with all the, shall we say, "imperfections" that a normal member of the public may have in an everyday situation. This isn't denigrating any member of the public, but you must appreciate that us voice-overs get to read in a pretty artificial way, and then after recording, our voices are processed again in an artificial way, where even breaths are often edited out and the final recording would be compressed or manipulated in other ways. So here are my tips as to how to sound like an "ordinary" person.

Most people sound much different between when they're adlibbing, in other words, making stuff up, when they're chatting between each other; and from when they're reading from a script or a book. In everyday life, it's generally no issue. In fact, young children like being read to at story time in an exaggerated "Once Upon A Time" way to overemphasise diction and learning points. It helps children learn new words. That's fine.

But if you're auditioning in this manner, delivering a script to an ad agency to voice a network TV script, where you're supposed to be a "man or woman in the street" you'll be thrown out after the first line. To speak naturally and not like you're just reading words off the script is a skill that all voice actors need to learn to do.

You see, if it sounds like you're reading, even though everyone knows that you really ARE reading from a script, it's a big no-no in the world of voiceover. And of course, TV presenters and news readers who are reading teleprompters in the studio also need to sound natural.

I'll share some techniques with you soon, but the problem is that, even if you follow these, you'll get into difficulties – we all do - particularly in directed sessions when endless takes of exactly the same words are demanded of you.

I'm sure you have been in advertising agency directed sessions, where there are a group of agency executives and maybe also representatives from the clients all arguing about the direction of your voice style, so they ask you down your headphones for ever more takes to try out subtle changes to the exact same words in front of you.

And that freshness and natural feel of the read at take 29 wears off fast, doesn't it? The weird thing is that some voice overs who really sound like they are reading, don't actually realise it.

So here's a very valuable test you can do. Record yourself when you're with a friend. Now ask your pal to ask you a really random question like "what did you think of the film on TV last night" or "why did you choose your car" or something like that. It needs to be a surprise, random question that you couldn't have prepared for. Play back the recording and transcribe it. In other words, write out what you said in your ad-libbed reply to your friend word for word, even writing down the stumbles and gasps in the right places, then start the recorder again.

This time you need to read your actual words again, but this time from the script. Now you'll have two recordings. So do you notice the differences between the two recordings? The main difference is, I think you'll find will be of the natural imperfections in the first one. And that's good. Humans are imperfect. We have characters, we have personalities, we have moods, we have emotions...we have breath.

These A.I. enhanced "text to speech" computer programmes that are supposed to take over the jobs of us voiceover artists can't do what we do. And computers will never be as good as us humans, certainly not in our lifetimes. The computer voice is just too perfect now to sound natural when reading a script.

I am not suggesting that you stumble all over it and leave gaps and breathe in the wrong places and so on. But a small but important amount of "intelligent imperfection" sprinkled into your performance will vastly improve the sound of it to the target audience and in particular to the ad agency or end client who hopefully will be convinced that they are listening to a natural acting performance, and not a voiceover reading a script.

Go back to the transcript that you got from answering your friend's question, and try and write in these imperfections. Maybe putting brackets where you left a bit of a gap, even put in breath marks. Try and put down on screen or your piece of paper the way you actually said it in a completely adlibbed style. And now of course, you've got to take it from the script and speak it again and try and get that adlibbed feel from the printed word. Now record another take, trying to emulate the original completely natural ad-libbed response.

So, now what do you do when you get a script that somebody else has written? First of all, like all good voice actors, you need to get into the head of the character. What is their age, what is their back story, why are they in that situation, what are they feeling right now, what is their relationship to the person they are talking to? Then read the script like you're THAT character.

You'll find yourself smiling as you speak while you become naturally serious in other parts. If you're allowed to change the script to localise it more with contractions, then please do it. So, for example, you'd say "aren't" rather than "are not" and so on. You may add sighs and deep breaths and "thinking pauses" which is probably what you found you did answering your friend's random questions.

Now, if it's not happening for you, naturally, don't worry. Just go through the script, mark it up. You'd underline key words to emphasise, you'd mark in pauses and take out pauses where it looks like one thought could suddenly and naturally jerk excitedly into the next. Some people end one sentence with the first word of the next, then leave a pause. Does your character do this?

Hopefully, the advertising agency or the production company would have given you details of who you are trying to play, whether a "young father or mother", a "boss" at work, a "garage attendant", a "police officer", or whatever, and then you can make it more natural and steer yourself away from the stereotype.

Here's a tip when you first get the script sent to you. If you see that you're about to open a script that's meant to be acted naturally, read the instructions, find out all about the character and the situation and the emotion, but don't even focus on the actual words of the script. Slam your machine into record and just read it aloud as soon as you see it. Make it a surprise. Now I know this sounds really crazy to say, but this is a technique that works for me, and many other voiceovers I know.

Start the recorder, and only then look at the words keeping in mind the character that you are meant to be. The reason for this, is that you don't want to sound too practised. And you will make a few stumbles maybe, and some natural sounding gaps between the words. Does it sound "natural"? That first recording can be a good reference of a natural read that you can refer to if you really have lost the will to live after the 30th take!

Another tip - be physical when recording. You won't believe how important this is to voice acting until you do it properly, and you'll then hear the difference. In most cases, nobody can see you, don't be embarrassed, so move around and "feel" the passion that you should feel, physically act the script, just give it your all, as you punch the air for the emphasis words and toss your head with a flourish for the final pay-off of the script. Just don't hit the microphone or wander off too far "off-mike"!

You won't need to do this as much if it's an informational script or eLearning or a phone prompt, but, honestly, don't be afraid of moving around and using your hands and arms to help flow and structure. This "physicality" I suggest when you are recording voiceovers, is very important and make the difference between an OK voiceover recording and a brilliant one. In fact, if you have a difficult turn of phrase or a long sentence where you can't really take a breath, moving and rolling your arms gently as if you are describing what you are saying will often help you. If you don't believe me, try it!

Finally, if you're asked to play the part of someone who is interviewed on video, in another language, this is somewhere else where you need to sound natural. If a boss of a factory in Germany for example, is talking about how wonderful his farm machinery company is, and you are doing the English translation pasted over the top of his voice, not in sync of course, then you don't want to sound like a "voice-over" delivering a finance ad do you?

So, put yourself in that person's position, and put on a proud corporate voice, you wouldn't put on the accent of that person's nationality normally, and that should be what the client would be looking for.

You need to sound like you ARE the proud owner of the company that is featured in your corporate script; or that you ARE the inventor of the product featured … you need to totally and utterly "own" the script, and be passionate about the content, and read in a style and speed that is suitable to the script and your character, and of course get these "paste-over" voiceovers to fit the original language version on the video!

16
VOICE MODULATION

"Modulation" is a posh way of saying how much melody we put into our voices. Without all important modulation, voices sound boring, monotone, and without much power or influence. Human beings do not communicate effectively in a monotone. They also don't communicate effectively by the way, speaking too fast, and the proof of both of those facts can be heard every day on commercial radio stations. TV and cinema commercials can put up "legal lines" about terms and conditions and so on as captions. On radio of course, there are no captions!

Listen to any radio commercial that has a legal line at the end, and most of the time it is spoken very fast and in a monotone. The reason this is done, is so psychologically you don't "hear" it. You don't take it in. The advertisers don't want you to hear it, it is only there because the law says it has to be there . "Terms and conditions apply, you will not own the car, cheques will not be honoured, full details on our website" etc.

So if you find it difficult to engage others with your speech, whether it's chatting to co-workers or chatting UP someone you fancy, it could be that you ARE speaking too fast and in too monotone a fashion!   It doesn't take that much effort to break out of this though.

Generally for documentary voiceovers, we are asked to go DOWN at the end of every sentence, because this is the traditional documentary style. This is the way narrators traditionally speak in a documentary.

Now generally, in Western culture, when we want to say a question, we go UP at the end of a sentence, sometimes like a little glide. It helps the communication process, and us voiceover artists are "communicators".

Just take the words away, and listen to the notes as if it was a song. That's the test to see if you are going up or staying the same, or even going down. If you say a question going down at the end it just doesn't make any sense at all or you sound like a robot.

Now many people I have met that speak in a monotone voice, seem to have developed this style, because they feel that it is cool or "gothic" to do so. But it's not really, and makes it very hard for the majority of people to actually understand what they're saying, and to fully engage. I'm not saying that you should learn to speak like a super animated "Radio DJ" type from the 1980s, because that would be really ridiculous, but to be honest, there are some certain traits from that style of speaking which you could take in very small amounts, and add it to a monotone voice, and that will give you much more power, and help you communicate your scripts in a more effective way. Not just that, but there are many clients who actually still want voiceover scripts read in this way. Honestly!

17
MID-ATLANTIC
OR "INTERNATIONAL" ACCENT

You're welcome to look up the history of this strange mélange of British R.P. (Received Pronunciation) and the General American accent; basically it was developed in the first part of the 20ᵗʰ Century when movies with sound were developed and US producers were worried that British people would not understand the strong American "twang", and British film makers were concerned too that their films with a posh British sound would not be understood by their colonial cousins the other side of the Atlantic! Modern day examples of this "Mid-Atlantic", "Transatlantic" or "International" accent, can be heard with the Crane brothers in Frazier, the Effie Trinket character in the Hunger Games, or Mr Burn's character in the Simpsons. When commercial radio started in the 1970's in the UK, many radio DJ's thought it cool to sound "American", so developed their own sound similar to this accent as well.

At an extremely simplified level, and speech experts will hate me for saying this, but all us British voiceovers really have to do is try to "sound a bit American" and "sound a bit British" if they are native North American.

General tips I was taught as a British person to sound American included using the "Stopped glottal T" so "button" would sound like "buddon" or "international" would sound like "indernational", and also tucking the chin in a bit to prevent projecting from the front; but you're welcome to take speech lessons to really nail this if it is important to you. The **21accents.com** site could be a good place to start if you're serious about acting accents.

Many clients in my experience are extremely lenient over this accent; all they want is for the communication to be delivered effectively for a "global" audience. If the budget doesn't stretch to separate British and US/Canadian versions of projects, then Mid-Atlantic is usually the way to go. Many English speakers who have been taught in the middle and Far East will have been trained probably by Americans so a British accent may sound very "posh".

An English listener may feel that a pure US accent is talking about something that's just not for them, particularly in a commercial, unless they are a well known and loved celebrity.

There is only one rule with this International Accent really, and that is, unless the client tells you otherwise, that whichever side of the Atlantic you are on, the pronunciations should all be North American. So, "Detail", "Process", "Leisure" and so on should NOT be said the way they are said in "BBC" or "RP" English.

If you're a British native, here are some guidelines:

Word	American pronunciation advice
schedule	The "ch" is pronounced as /k/ - this is becoming a British way now
leisure	LEE-zure
progress	The "o" sounds like the /a/ sound as in "want"
Tuesday	first syllable sounds like "too"
knew/new	rhymes with "too"
tomato	"a" sounds like "a" in debate
vase	rhymes with "lace"
privacy	1st syllable "pri" sounds like "pry"
vitamin	1st syllable "vit" rhymes with "bite"
water	War-duhr
again	Rhymes with "ten"
basket	"a" as in "cat"
process	Prah-sess
bath	"a" as in "cat"
z (letter of the alphabet)	Sounds like "zee"

Words with Different Stressed Syllables in American vs. British English:

Word	American pronunciation with stressed syllable capitalized:
adult	uh-DULT
advertisement	AD-ver-tize-ment
ballet	ba-LAY
buffet	buh-FAY
caffeine	kaf-EEN
café	kaf-AY
chauffeur	show-FUR
controversy	KON-truh-ver-see
debut	day-BYOO
detail	Der-TAIL
garage	guh-RAZH
gourmet	gor-MAY
ice cream	ICE kreem
mobile (adjective)	MO-bill
montage	MON-tazh
nonchalant	non-shu-LAHNT
premature	pree-muh-CHURE
princess	PRIN-sess
salon	sa-LON
Thanksgiving	thanks-GIVE-ing
vaccine	vaks-EEN
weekend	WEEK-end

18

COLOURING AND SHOWCASING WORDS

With many scripts, unless it's a character voice read or you are actually asked specifically for a "monotone" or "mystic / poetic" read, look for opportunities to _colour_ words to make the script more interesting, easier on the ear and to have more "selling power" in promos and commercials.

Have you ever heard of the word "Onomatopoeia"? The official definition is "the formation of a word from a sound associated with what is named (e.g. _cuckoo_, _sizzle_)" but of course saying those words in THAT way, isn't playing the game, as you should speak these words as the associated sound ...sounds!

But for us voice artists, we take this one step further as we can colour words that DON'T HAVE any sound associated with it, like BEAUTIFUL. In commercials you will get a big thank you from the client if you describe his or her products as "BEAUTIFUL" with real emotion as if you are describing something or some service as actually "beautiful".

You often have to think of something that is "of the word" so you can naturally speak the word with that subtle but very important enhancement. It's our job to make words come alive when it's appropriate. Even if words don't have emphasis on them, saying the words in a "colourful" way really can make even an average script sound wonderful with a good voiceover in charge. The key, as I've alluded to, is to think of the meaning and that will give you a clue as to what the sound should be. "Treacle" shouldn't really be said as a bright sound in an upper register, unless you're selling it, maybe, it should have a gloopy, heavy dark sound. The word "perky" should sound "perky" as well! I'm sure you get the drift of all this.

Remember nobody can see you as a voiceover so feel free to move around to feel the emotion as long as you don't go off-mike or you hit the microphone, or rustle too much in your clothing. Lose your inhibitions! Have fun!

So here are a list of words - just have a go yourself. Record yourself and play back as always afterwards. So here are some ordinary monochrome words...see how much colour you can put into them!

CRUMBLE	AMAZING	HUGE
CARESS	HIT	CREEP UP
SMASH	FORCE	SEXY
ANNILIATE	GURGLE	SPLASH
REGURGITATE	HONK	BOING!
GIGGLE	BLURT	WHISPER

Now there may be a word you've coloured very well, but just needs to be a little bit more emphasised, and it's a technique called "showcasing" where basically you put a little gap before and a little gap after a word or a short group of words and you increase the volume a little bit as well.

You do this in commercials a lot usually for the client's name or for a phone number or web address or something like that.   I know there are many clients who like every word to be "showcased" - but of course, when everything is emphasised, nothing is then emphasised. But try saying that to a client.

So, in a directed session, if a client asks for the client's name to be "showcased", you'll know what they mean!

19
RECORDING LISTS IN SCRIPTS

Some years ago in the United Kingdom, when the train companies got rid of live railway announcements at stations, they brought in an automated system, and a friend of mine got the job to record every station name in the United Kingdom.

But he had to do them all twice.

In case a train "terminated" or finished its journey at a certain station he had to say the name not just sounding like as part of a list that was continuing, but the END of a list - so in other words, the word would come down at the end with a sense of finality.

So it was a pretty boring job, reading all those place names out in England, Wales and Scotland, but at least he got paid twice for the different versions of the names! Dear voiceover Phil Sayer passed away some years ago, but they still use his recordings on the London Underground, as the "Mind The Gap" announcement, and still in many train stations across the UK, and it shows that as a voiceover, you can become immortal!

The learning point is how lists need to be tackled. But particularly if your list is in a video script voice over, you need to know how they are going to edit it in the final product. Are they going to show a shot or a few shots of each of the specific processes that you are listing? Or are they showing lots of general shots, where your words in the list can run into each other? You see if the former, you need to give a good gap between each word in the list so they can expand it as necessary in the edit suite to fit the pictures illustrating what you are saying in the list.

If the latter, in other words, where they HAVEN'T any specific shots to go with your list, it would sound terrible to separate the terms or items. This is where you almost casually roll one item into the next. "Yeah, we got this, we got that"-kind of attitude. But this is where you need to talk to the client to find out where the list is going to be used and to maybe look at the video that's edited already.

When you get experienced in voice over, you can get into "list mode " pretty quickly, if you can see one coming up. This is as long as the client has bothered to put the punctuation points in correctly of course. If you see words with commas in the corner of your eye coming up in the next sentence or two when you are sight reading a script, that's when to get ready for list mode, and then when you see the full stop or the period, that's the end word with the sense of finality , where you always come down in tone at the end.

20
DEALING WITH BREATHS

I was reading an article about artificial intelligence and how computers are going to take over our work as voice over artists, and I have more thoughts on this later, but it was particularly amusing to read that the developers are having to add in "artificial breaths" to make their computer voices more realistic. Which is strange isn't it, as us voiceovers do our best to minimise breaths and for some types of script, spend ages cutting them out in edit afterwards. An area where you can speed up your editing is not to spend so much time on your breaths unless you really have to do this work. I know voice over artists who are obsessed by cutting out every instant of every breath in every type of recording, as if they are highly embarrassed about them. However, there are different ways of approaching editing or adjusting breaths, and it all depends on the type of script it is and the kind of use it's going to have.

If you are recording a radio or TV commercial, almost certainly the paucity of time you have, and the usually over-written scripts you are given, will mean that breaths will have to be cut out completely. Audiences are used to hearing the artificial sound of a fast voiceover on a commercial, where there is no time for the luxury of breathing. This is really the only place where virtually every voice over script needs to have its breaths cut out completely.

When I mean cut out, I mean just that you would highlight the breath on the audio waveform in Adobe Audition or whatever - push delete - and the two sides come together. This reduces the duration of the full file, but it sounds really artificial, because in real life, a human being has to breathe.

The other side of the coin is natural acting, where you wouldn't touch the breaths at all. You wouldn't process the sound either by compression, EQ or noise gate, and you would leave all the breaths in, in fact quite often that's part of the acting experience, and you would just leave everything alone.

So what about the other types of voice job then? What would you do with the breaths then? You may still have a script with a timing issue even for something like a corporate video where you're trying to fit your voice over with a non-English original narration that's been translated.

But usually, for a straight narration without any timing issues whatsoever, it sounds wrong to cut out breaths and butt up words against each other. It sounds artificial, and it hinders the listeners appreciation and understanding of what you are trying to communicate.

You could use a **hardware** Noise Gate device that cuts out breaths as you record, but I really don't recommend this as it will sense breaths and simply cut the volume at these points to zero which sounds awful, especially for listeners on headphones, hearing all these little sections of complete silence pepper the recording. Unless you are recording a separate version WITH breaths, you also won't have an "original" version to play with afterwards either. The software noise gate in Adobe Audition is extremely sensitive, but I don't use it for the same reason. You set the threshold and cuts to zero the level on the breaths. Sounds terrible.

So the best way to deal with breaths, if you really feel they are distracting, is to reduce their volume. So, in other words you would highlight each breath and you would reduce the volume, by using a keyboard shortcut to save time.

My personal shortcut is the keyboard "F" key. And usually if I reduce each breath by about 10 to 15 decibels, that still keeps the breath there in the background so it all sounds natural, and the timing hasn't changed at all, again making it sound like real conversation, but the sound and volume of the breath isn't as distracting.

There are automated ways of doing this, via a great "soft" noise gate plug in from Reason, called the Reagate. The Reagate is free to download at the time of writing. Just open it up, and then "search for plug-ins" in the Adobe Addition plug in manager. It has a lovely "pre-sensing" feature and even separate wet and dry faders so the noise gate doesn't cut off the starts of soft words that start with "s" for example. The Reagate works well as an automated "soft noise gate", but if it's an important script and you've been paid well, and you need a perfect job, then there is no option but to reduce the volume manually for every breath, I'm afraid.

Of course, you could just leave your breaths in, and maybe the end client won't notice, or be distracted by them, but I think if you have pride in your work, and you want to impress the client, you will want to create as clean a recording for them as possible.

So how can you make your breathing less distracting in the first place? I assume that you try to keep yourself as physically fit as possible, and if you have any breathing medical issues, you use your medications. For example, I am a mild asthmatic, and I have to use my inhalers a couple of times a day and my blue ones when I have an asthma attack, so do whatever the doctor tells you, eat healthily, drink lots of fresh water to keep hydrated, do cardio exercise every day, and all the usual healthy advice that you read in magazines.

Now in life, you should always breathe through your nose, because the air gets filtered that way, but in the voice booth, behind the microphone, it's fine to breathe through an open mouth, because that way breathing noise is a minimised. It's a bit of a technique to do, and you look a bit strange, but remember nobody can see you doing a voice over recording can they? And that thought is even more important if you're going to consider this next tip.

Firstly, hold your nose and speak, and you sound a bit like a demented puppet don't you? Is extremely nasal of course. So if you haven't got a cold and you can breathe through your nose you sound "normal".

But what if you could increase the amount of air that goes through your nose? And that's of course what those strips of springy metal do that you stick on your nose that widen the passages. You get them from pharmacies or buy them from Amazon. Look for "breathe easy nasal strips" – quite a few people make them. People use them in bed, to stop them snoring, because it opens up the nasal passages only slightly, but it makes all the difference between breathing properly in bed and opening your mouth and snoring all night.

But us voice overs can use these in the voice booth and I use these particularly for very soft, intimate voice overs especially when I'm being directed and I can't stop and start, they want to hear the whole read in one go, and I really need to minimise my breathing and use every atom of oxygen I can get in cleanly without making a noise through the nose.

Yes, you do look ridiculous, and pretty pig-like as if you're from Royston Vasey, but, hey we're voice actors and nobody can see us, can they?! The angle you put these on is pretty critical, you put them on the bridge of the nose then angle them down so that it opens your nose as effectively as possible.

For some people, these things are an absolute miracle, and you just feel yourself breathing cleanly and more effectively than you ever have before. Even if you don't need these in the voice booth often, try them in bed, because if you can sleep with your mouth fully closed all night, that's great, because it means that your voice doesn't get dried out in the night.

Two more breathing tips. If you can stand up in the voice booth rather than sit down, this will maximise your breathing potential, as well as to teach yourself to breathe from the diaphragm, so you fully fill those lungs of yours.

Finally - we often get scripts with sentences that are ridiculously long so this is where you need to use the "stop and start" technique.

This is where you identify a long sentence, and you keep going till there's an edit point, where you know you'll be able to chop out a huge breath later without anybody knowing. This will usually be at a comma. So take your obvious big gasp of air, really obvious so you'll see it easily in edit afterwards, and then carefully chop out the gasp. This technique will only work if in recording after your gasp, you start off again with your full lung capacity at the same volume and energy level as you left it with when you were running out of air or it will sound like an edit. Try it . It's a great technique.

21
MOUTH CLOSURE

When people talk in real life, they normally close their mouths completely at the end of every sentence, and sometimes in the middle of sentences; it can only be for milliseconds, but it's an important thing to note for us voiceovers. It's because when a microphone is very close to our mouths, that subtle little lip smack doesn't sound that attractive, and it's just emphasised because of the closeness of the microphone.

So a technique that voice artists have to learn is to not to close their mouths when recording. This "lip smack" is often extremely subtle, and is often unnoticeable if you have dry lips, it's never going to be as bad as the pesky donkey in the Shrek movie, but just try noticing if your lips do touch, and when you're aware of it, just stop doing it! Now, when you record yourself, you'll find your recordings subtly cleaner.

In my opinion, here are three important times when you SHOULD keep your mouth closed in life. First of all, when you're outside, by traffic or other air pollution, close your mouth so the air is filtered via your nasal cavities, so your precious vocal equipment isn't irritated.

Secondly, keep that mouth shut if you're near anyone who looks like they're ill or sneeze near you, and then thirdly at night in bed, keep your mouth closed, because if you sleep with your mouth open, then this dries out your vocal folds terribly. If you're a kind of sleeper who wakes up regularly in the night, then have a glass of water that you can have a sip of before you go back for another spell of sleep, but if you sleep right through, you can train yourself not to have your mouth open.

As mentioned before in the Breaths section, a medical device you may like to investigate are the self-adhesive strips that are made of bendy springy plastic that you place over the soft part of your nose. These keep your nostrils open wider than they would normally be, and help you to breathe better in the night. Search for Nasal Strips or Breath Easy strips. I use them in the voice booth as well for very softly spoken scripts to minimise the sound of breathing.

22
CHECKING PRONUNCIATIONS

For scripts that you record without any direction, it's so important that you check pronunciations before you start. You may record the most wonderful performance and it may be technically brilliant, but if you just get one name incorrectly pronounced, then it's "fixit" time. Of course, it's not just names of places and people, you also have to know from the client whether they want the British or American pronunciation of words. You may think this is obvious with the accent of the voice talent chosen, in other words, you, but it's not.

As someone who is British and lives in the UK, I have very many clients in The United States, who love my British accent for certain projects, however they want me to say American words like process, leverage, leisure, etc. in the North American way, and of course the client is always right! But that's not always true, so it's always best to check first.

As for names, we are so lucky with the Internet that we can quite often check the correct pronunciation of a name within a few seconds. If it's a company name, then I tend to go onto YouTube and type in that name and add the word "interview", this way I'm more likely to find a news report where someone from that organisation is being interviewed, so you should get the correct pronunciation from that.

If you find a corporate image video from the company, quite often it's just music all the way through and you don't hear the name of the company spoken! So search for "interview" or "report" on YouTube. For place names, and in particular if you are doing a tourist information guide, you need to find out if you are meant to speak in the native language, or the British equivalent.

There have been arguments about this for years, for example, in France, Paris is called "Par-ee". Yet in an English script, "Paris" is simply called "Paris", isn't it?

So for smaller place names, or descriptions of areas, names of churches, or anything like this, should you say it the local way, or the anglicized way? Here is where the school of "the client is always right" comes into play. I have to ask this question so many times as I record a lot of tourist audio guides, I have a whole paragraph of boiler plate available on my Autotext software, that I customise for email enquiries, before I record anything.

Although YouTube is the best place to find the correct pronunciation of organisations and company names, it is pretty useless for any other type of pronunciation, the people who make these awful videos showing you how to pronounce one word, pad out the video with so much nonsense, just to make it as long as possible so they get more advertising revenue, and to add insult to injury, when they eventually say the actual word, quite often they get the pronunciation wrong anyway!

So for people's names and place names, spoken by a native tongue, and not by a computer, I recommend **www.Forvo.com**. For English language words for both British and American pronunciation, I use **www.howjsay.com**. If it's a low budget quick and dirty script where you have to give it your best guess, and there's nothing on those two sites, then Google Translate can be a life saver. However, for the best results, and the easiest thing to do, is to ask your client for an audio recording saying each of the unusual words very slowly, and for very difficult words, syllable by syllable.

Now, you may have spent a lot of time learning the phonetic way of writing pronunciations , and you will be screaming at me now saying why not use that? Well, the problem is that maybe the client doesn't quite know how to use the phonetic system properly, but they WILL know how to actually say the names, won't they? So ask them for a recording!

What I suggest you do is to make a copy of the script as a separate file, and strip out everything leaving just the unusual names that you need. Then get rid of the gaps, and you will end up with a list of names in the order that they appear in your script. You would send this list to the client, saying *"sorry I can't find out how to say these names definitively, would you mind recording them in a very quiet place, close to the microphone, and very slowly"*?

There are some languages where even with the client speaking slowly on your audio guide, it's difficult to understand how to say the words, and I find Polish, Russian and Arabic languages pretty difficult to understand, so I have friendly clients who helpfully say the words syllable by syllable, and then also say the word at the normal speed afterwards .

Don't ask the client to send you separate audio files. It's far easier just to have one file with all the pronunciations in the order they appear in the script. It will save you time and also save the time of the client having to put this together for you.

Once you get the pronunciation guide, you would open it in a separate playback software than the one you're using to recording, in fact you will have to won't you! What I do, is to have two copies of Adobe Audition open, a very old copy, that just plays the pronunciation guide, and then you record as usual on the up-to-date version of Adobe Audition.

Then you just keep recording on your new copy of Audition, and just ALT + TAB to listen to the next name when it comes up. Yes, you could play the pronunciation guide on a media player, or on good ol' VLC traffic cone player, but it's handy to see the actual waveform on the screen.

Finally, I'm sure I don't need to tell you this, but make sure when you're stopping to hear the pronunciation, that you record it so that when it's edited in, it will be completely seamless, so you'd get the tone of voice and volume matching either side of the "hole" where the name will be.

23
IMPROVING SIGHT READING SKILLS

Short scripts like radio ads or promos you can analyse and almost memorise. That's not the case for very long eLearning scripts, tourism guides or audiobooks. You may have skimmed through the manuscripts, but you will be effectively "sight-reading" as you record. The more you read aloud, and ideally also record and play back so you can monitor your performance so you can improve, the better you'll get at sightreading.

Of course, you'll always get some sentence construction or a missing punctuation issue where it's not obvious what the sense is, and you'll need to stop and pick up, but you need to get to a stage of being able to pick a random book on a shelf, open any page and start narrating to a very high standard.

The other advantage of reading more and more, is that your vocabulary will improve. Years ago, my boss at the radio station where I was a presenter at, thought I should expand my on-air vocabulary. He told me that I had to find a new word each day, write it in a book with its meaning and use it on that day's radio show, without it being obvious that I've slipped it in.

That tip has paid off so well over the years! So when you get to a word that an author has used that you're not quite sure how to say it or what it means, stop and use a pronunciation site like **Forvo.com** or **HowJSay.com**; but also click on the MEANING as well, as that will help you remember it for the future.

Another skill for the long-form script narrator is to understand English grammar. But why, you may say? Isn't that for the writer to sort out? Well, yes, but if you, the narrator, also understand English grammar to a high standard, you'll also know how you can break some grammar rules for speaking – conversational English is so different from formal written English - so if you need to brush up on your "subject" and "predicate" of a sentence; "clauses" and "parts of speech", then do so, as it will really help you in the long run.

What about the word "the"? Do you know when to say it as "THUR" and when you say "THEE"? Is "the" preceding a vowel? In which case it IS "THEE". Don't worry, with grammar, you'll get to a stage where you won't need to remember the actual rules, things will just "sound wrong", as you listen to your performance as you record.

At the end of the day, the narration should sound natural and pleasant for the listener to hear as well as being fully connected to the type of script that you're narrating. Ask yourself at all times: "If I were listening to this, would I relate to what's going on?" "Would I understand what is being narrated?" For a fiction audiobook, "Would I know which character is speaking now?"

The way you do this at all times, is to continually monitor yourself, using the "Third Head Technique" mentioned earlier.
Yes, you COULD of course play back everything you record on the loudspeakers to check after recording each chapter, but that would eat up a lot of time in your day. You can speed up your playback by pushing the "L" key on your keyboard when you are playing back in Adobe Audition, but it really does your head in listening to a double-speed voice over! Voiceovers need to be totally confident that what they've recorded is accurate and clear before sending files to clients.

Do you really want to send off chapters to your client and then have a long list of notes with mistakes and errors and omissions and bad pronunciations that all have to be fixed?

If you think just the recording and editing of long form voice work is tiring, just wait until you have to REPAIR your recordings - maybe weeks into the future when you've forgotten much of the project. If you find monitoring yourself difficult to master, try using headphones, listening to your voice without any latency or delay, at the same time that you're speaking.

If you've ever worked in the radio industry, you will have to wear headphones anyway, particularly when you're listening to what your producer is saying, without it coming on the air, or to deal with phone calls without feedback happening.

When you are a voice over, sometimes wearing headphones helps you enunciate better, because it amplifies the sound in your head. If you can't get on with wearing both ears on, try putting one headphone on the ear and the other one not on, and some people like this. But most people to be honest, can cope without headphones at all, and it's much more comfortable, especially for long recording sessions.

24
VOICE ACTING & CHARACTER VOICES

If you "just" want to be a narrator or jobbing voiceover artist, that's fine, but you may be leaving a lot of cash on the table. Learn the extra skills of voice acting and those extra strings to your bow could add a big new income stream.

Voiceovers or "voiceover artists" get scripts that need to be read in a variety of different styles, but it's still really your own voice. You could be asked to read in a corporate manner, a friendly and casual style, or in a "hard sell" style for commercials. And sometimes you may be asked to do some character voices.

So if you're a voice over who's never really tackled character voices at all yet, let's see if this can inspire you a little. It's an easy and fun way to do different types of voice work, and if you'd like to know more about this with regard to game, animation work or fiction audiobooks that need character voices and how to get work, check out my "Voice Acting" course on **www.VoiceoverMasterclass.com**.

Now, every one of us have got our own "base voice", which you would usually use as a "narrator" type voice for "'*yer every day voice work*". Consider the ways that you can change your voice in different situations. Like when you're screaming at your favourite sports team, talking to a small child, having a conversation with your boss, having an argument with someone, all the usual variations of human life where the voice changes.

Now can you add to that any interesting accents, or can you imitate any voices from cartoons, celebrities or public figures that you know? If you've not really done character work before, you just need to explore what you can or can't achieve and you need to fully strip away any shyness or feeling of self-consciousness.

There was a time when I didn't do much character voice work, but some years ago I needed to do a lot of fiction audio book work with lots of different characters in, and also happened to be offered a lot of indie game work, where I was paid to be three or four completely separate characters but they all appear in one game, so I had to think of a way how to make the characters different from each other. What I did was to create a sort of "control panel", that doesn't exist, that I could turn up and down for various characteristics that I was pretty good at doing.

You can try this as well, but your "controls" may be very different from mine. Just imagine your voice has separate controls that you can turn up and down and select different attributes. My own control panel has 10 separate "knobs" for: inherent personality, accent, shape of your mouth, register, nasality, overall physicality, emotion, power of the voice, the speed or pace of speaking, and a "clip control" which determines whether the voice is clipped or legato and smooth.

These changeable parameters are the ones that I have developed over the years for all the video game and audio book characters that I've recorded, and you're welcome to use this and adapt it and add to it for your own needs. And it's helped me enormously because you just need to work out what setting each control is on, and you've got a character voice.

Unfortunately, unlike electronic equipment where you can store settings as a pre-set, the human brain has to remember the voice and also refer to a sample recording, so that you can slip into each voice again next time the character comes up in the audiobook or game script. Let me go through each of those ten of my "controls" in turn.

PERSONALITY

If I gave you a list of types of personalities, probably, I bet in your mind a type of voice would already pop into your head. If I said "stuffy & pompous", you'll have an idea of this type of voice. A wide-eyed enthusiastic person may speak with great clarity and be very fast paced, and maybe jittery or nervous. So think about the personality of your character, and that's a good place to start for the voice that you could assign to them. What has the author or game producer told you about this character? How do they relate to the people around them?

ACCENT

Some people find picking up accents and sustaining them very easily, others can't handle them at all apart from some stereotypical style that you can get away with for comedy reads. First of all, identify the sounds and speech parts that are generally spoken differently by people from the area you are trying to sound like.

You need to identify the sounds that are specific to that accent. For example, if you are trying to do a German accent you must never sound the letter W. It's never Volkswagen, it's VolksVAGEN.

Also the word "the" often sounds like "ze" like Russians may do, as the "th" sound doesn't exist in their language. So if you are reading a script, you need to adjust the script to put these changes of sounds in. Then look at the tone colour of the accent or person. In English we generally speak in a flowing legato pattern with elongated word endings.

Still taking German as an example, they tend to speak with truncated endings, almost a staccato speech pattern and almost monotone. If you trying to do an Italian accent, it's the opposite; everything runs together with few gaps and loads of usual enthusiasm and hand gestures. If you're musical, it can help a lot by replacing words by notes in your heads like we mentioned before. Get the "tune" of the accent right and it will really help. By the way, hand gesture and anything physical when you are recording does help you to get the voice right!

Then play some videos of the person you are trying to emulate or of people using the accent you want to voice. You need to look at the mouth movements. How is the mouth used? If you're staring out, try and go for the stereotype first, then you can hone the accent and voice further into more subtleties . But the visual thing is very important, if you get the face and physical movements of the person you're trying to emulate in your head, it makes it so much easier.

So if you are trying to do a cockney accent, try and sound like a – and sorry for any offence here, cabbies - London cabbie, get that right, then soften that down. You'll notice many cockney sentences end with the mouth open. Whatever accent or impersonation you are going for, studying the mouth on its own with the volume down, gestures of hand, and the face can all help in honing to perfection the voice you want to emulate.

SHAPE
The shape of your mouth and your vocal apparatus can totally change the voice style. Try speaking where your end position is an open little circle, in other words you never close your mouth but always goes back to how you would say the sound OOOO. Just see how that kind of shape of mouth can change the speech that you make. Or try stretching your mouth very wide as if you were trying to say the letter E all the time, the shape of a post box. This I use for melodrama evil characters. Try speaking like that and see if that gives you the results you want for your character.

Another type of change you can make to your voice is by simply expanding your throat inside. Just yawn for me now - and just feel what's going on inside your neck area. And just keep it in a sort of half-yawn, and now speak. It sounds sort of mellow, and this could be a nice touch to add to a character who has a rather posh, affected voice, to make it sound different from someone else. If they have an awful lot of words to read, I wouldn't suggest doing this, because it does hurt to keep this semi-yawn for any amount of time.

And don't forget that all these different shapes can then be mixed with whatever you selected on the accent control and the other controls that we've giving you here. So experiment, record yourself, and playback, but don't forget that clarity is key. And if you find it hard to get into that character and to stay there, only use those sort of voices, for minor characters.

REGISTER
Have you heard of the registers of the voice? The "Laringeal Mechanisms" to give them the technical name. Different physiological adjustments of larynx enable the wide range of frequencies of the human voice; it's all very clever. This is the way we can adjust the vocal tract to give all the huge variations of vocal qualities and timbres of our speaking and singing voices.

The vocal folds are named from zero to three (M0, M1, M2 and M3), each associated with lower to higher tones. Each of these membranes, the vocal folds, have differing lengths and thickness. M0 creates a low and nasty, creaky "vocal fry" sound. It's your human "sub-woofer" speaker in a way, no power, but it adds depth to the overall voice. Just use this M0 vocal fold on its own, and you'll soon get a sore throat. Most speech for men and women is using the M1 and M2 folds. The upper end of that and into M3 gets into falsetto territory. Really skilled vocalists are switching on and off these 4 layers, whether they know they're actually doing it or not.

That's the weird thing about creating voices. A doctor can say what's technically going on down there, but for us voice actors, we need to use psychological techniques to switch on and off the vocal fold layers to get the voice we want or need. For many actors, after lots of experimentation, they get the voice and then use a trigger word or catch phrase to get back into that voice, or think of an actual person, or look at a picture. Impersonators often use this technique.

NASALITY
As well as working on the basic vibrations of the vocal folds, you could also add in nasality, by lowering or raising the soft palate. I'll give you this trick again - simply hold your nose and say AAH. Nothing happens. Now hold your nose and go "HANGGGGG". Wow! That's a difference! You're sending the air up the nose that you're now blocking. You're moving your soft palate, which is really the back door to the nose, up and down. Keep the soft palate down and you get a nasal sound, usually not wanted in rich voiceover work, but could be great for a character voice, especially mixed with an accent!

PHYSICALITY
Just by moving your arms around and emphasising certain words and pulling yourself back and standing in a certain way and moving closer and further away from the microphone can totally change your voice, and really assist you in getting through difficult scripts.

So with characters, try moving around in a jaunty way, or move your head at a strange angle and try speaking like that. Or pretend that you're in pain while you're speaking.....squeeze yourself in..... honestly it's amazing how many different types of character voices can come along when you just experiment. Just have fun, and record some voices and see what happens. Remember nobody can see you in the voice booth, so if any kind of physicality helps you to achieve and to sustain a voice character, then just do it!

EMOTION
So, at that point in the audiobook story, or video game, or cartoon, is it obvious the character is really upset, or angry, or wants to persuade the other character to do something? The sort of emotion you choose for each character at each part in the book really comes with understanding where you are in the story and for each

character you really have to get into their shoes. How would they be affected by what's going on around them? Why would they speak in this way? Nailing down the right emotion at the right time will really make your characters sound much more authentic.

POWER
The power of voice includes volume and also can be wrapped up with emotion as we've mentioned before, and you may have some people who speak very softly, and expect to be heard, or they could be softly speaking to themselves, almost like a mumble. And you may get an author who asked you to mumble some lines, but try and keep in mind the poor listener who does have to make out the words that you are saying, because they don't have the text in front of them!   If you are in the voice booth and about to do some really loud lines, such as shouting at the top of your voice, remember to check back the loud section as soon as you've done it, in case you have over modulated, and have distorted the recording. Maybe you would like to experiment with recording the loud lines with the input to your computer or recording device at a slightly lower setting.

SPEED
Some people speak very fast and enthusiastically, and that's fine, but again, remember to keep the clarity in the speech! And some people speak ridiculously slowly. Now speed is very useful to you if you have two or three characters who all have the same accent, that is different from your main narrator accent, and it's a way that, if you can only do one type of foreign accent, you can differentiate the characters from each other. One person could speak faster or slower than the other one.

CLIP
The clip control determines how legato the voice is. Some people speak in a very joined up manner, sounding like treacle or rich honey emanating from their mouths enjoying the resonance of each word flow into the next. Whereas other people have a very clipped

voice, where the beginnings and ends are completely separate, and you could almost hear the slight pauses between each one, and certainly between the beginnings and ends of sentences.

So by taking a look at the list of controls that you can adapt yourself, you can switch some controls off - you can have some on full - you can have some on medium and all sorts of different character voices can begin to create themselves, and then you would write down what these parameters are, and of course make sample recordings for your character voice library.

Well, have fun experimenting with your own vocal control panel. Don't forget that if you learn a new skill on one of the categories, for example you learn how to do a new accent, suddenly you can add that to any of the other parameters so your amount of available characters goes up.

I'm often asked about "other sex" voices when it comes to characters. If you're a man, of course you don't need to impersonate a woman's generally higher voice, or you'll end up in comedy Monty Python land. Simply take the resonance out, sound softer, raise the tone slightly and that will be fine for a man voice actor representing a woman character voice. The other way round, as well as lowering the pitch, women can sound manly by adding a bit of "gruff" or a pinch of a regional accent...you need to experiment! But don't worry too much about this. If you're a male narrator in an audiobook, and say "Barbara looked her friend and said..." or whatever, the listener is expecting to hear a female speaking anyway, so their brain will compensate!

Some people find picking up accents and sustaining them very easily, others can't handle them at all apart from some stereotypical style that you can get away with for comedy reads. But as with everything in life, practise makes perfect, and as well as trying to achieve the character voice you want, you need to also get consistency, so every time your character appears in the game, or in the audio book, it sounds authentic and consistent.

25
AUDIOBOOK WORK

The world of audiobooks is greatly expanding, and that's something not many industries can boast of at the moment! In fact, the Audio Publishers Association of America have reported for the 8th year in a row, double-digit revenue growth. This year, audiobook sales just in the United States brought in 1.2 billion dollars, and that's up 16% in sales this year. The great thing is that there's still plenty of room for expansion in the audiobook market because it's still a small part of the total book sales, but audiobooks are actually getting more and more important in people's lives these days, as well as podcasts. It seems that in the post-pandemic days, us humans just need to hear even more other humans talk and discuss things and tell us stories.

We've all got more stress and hassle than ever these days, and enjoying an audiobook is a sort of oasis, a secret place and special world where people can escape to. Yes, an audiobook is such a great medium to enjoy when you're out for a walk, in a gym, on a long journey in a car, or travelling on a train, it helps people absorb a story or a factual book that they are interested in, to escape the crazy world for a while with their earbuds or headphones on.
 In general, people are loving audio experiences more these days anyway, as there is less time to sit down to consume television; radio listening is going up and so is listening to podcasts which is another huge growth area.

I've been a voiceover and narrator over 40 years. My love of recording audio books comes from my narration work in TV documentaries, and from understanding how important the narrator is to carry the viewer along the structure of the program. The interesting thing is, that when the pictures are taken away from a television documentary into an audio only format, it is the skill of the narrator to actually create those missing pictures in the listener's head, turning the expert words of the author into sound. Before recording, you as the narrator, would have at least skim-read through the book, and have got a sense of where it is going, and you would have of course the text in front of you on the screen as you record it. For listeners, they have only your voice in their head to follow what's going on, so not only does the vocal delivery need to be crystal clear, but you need to let the sense of what you're saying sink in.

So why aren't all audiobooks narrated by the actual authors? Well for most of the classics, it's rather difficult for these authors to narrate anything – er, because they're dead; but for contemporary books, audio versions that are read by the actual author are rare; it's not always that authors haven't the skills or the right kind of voice, often it's because they feel out of their comfort zone in a recording studio, or maybe they haven't the time to record as the pressure is on to write their next project!

So that leaves a lot of work for us, voice actors, but the first thing we'd say to you is to make sure you have the time to devote to audiobook recording. You need to be committed, dedicated and professional and not be prone to distraction. Even for a short story audio book of say, an hour, you are looking at a good 2 hours or more of solid work, and more if it's a factual technical or medical book where you have to stop regularly to check pronunciations, or if it's a fiction project full of different character voices. You can't "just knock off 10 minutes' worth" before breakfast and come back to it later. Your voice will change, your mood will change, the different sections won't edit together successfully, trust me, they really won't.

Let me sum up the whole audiobook production process: First, as we know, there are two types of audiobooks, in the same way as there are two types of books; fiction or non-fiction, or as I call them, "factual". The audiobook process is in three parts – the three "P's" – PREPARATION, PERFORMANCE & PRODUCTION.

The Preparation work includes agreeing the fee, choosing the narrator if you're a producer not voicing it yourself, choosing the voice styles for the characters and then adapting the whole manuscript for audio use. This may mean cutting chunks out that don't make sense in an audio format as visuals or photos are discussed or changing the text so it does.

The Performance is the recording process itself with the narrator. For bigger budget audiobooks, often the narrator will be just that; the producer or director will cast the most appropriate voice talent, they'd work with the author to adapt the original print or Kindle version for audio use, and the voice actor will be directed in the studio for the recording sessions.

After the recording, the hired voice goes away and it's up to the producer and their team of editors and mixers to get the final product that consumers will get to listen to via one of the many audiobook platforms.

For smaller budgets, it is perfectly possible for it to be a one-person job, to get the manuscript from the author, adapt it for audio in association with the author, to record it and to edit and master the files, all to a very high standard, and all from the comfort of your own home, and all done by you.

So, if it's you wearing all the hats, and that's the way we like to work, actually, you'll not just be narrating, but also be responsible for editing and mastering the recorded material in the Production part of the three "P" part process.

26
GETTING PAID FOR AUDIOBOOK NARRATION

If you're just getting into understanding character voices, or even starting voice over work itself, recording audio books is a good way to start. You might like doing just factual or non-fiction books which is fine - they are basically enormously long documentary type scripts, although there may be some character quotes in some factual books; but where your character work will really come alive will be in FICTION books, where quite often, there are different characters interacting with each other. Because the listener cannot see the text of the book or the script in front of them, you have to make it very clear as to who is talking to who.

You also have to learn good technical production techniques. Why is this important? Well, if you hire a studio , or studio hires you as "just a narrator", you really won't have much cash to take home at the end of the day for an audiobook.

The average fee "per finished hour" – that's an hour of edited together material, not the time it took you to get this edited recording - to just narrate an average "non-name" audio book can be not great – just $75 to $150 per finished hour. But if you learn the skills to actually edit together the files after recording, in other words "produce" the audiobook as well, you can ask for $150 to $350 per finished hour, especially if you have a decent and fair author and/or publisher.

The work is more satisfying as well if you don't just narrate it, but edit it and master it as well. This is called "audiobook production" and so basically clients would hire you as a narrator and a producer together. People with these joint skills are much more valuable in the world of the audio book, and if you are a narrator AND producer, you could either get contacted direct from authors or publishers, or you can work on one of the many audiobook platforms we'll discuss later.

Assuming you are a freelance narrator and have been approached by an author or publisher, you need to ascertain two main things:
How much you'll be paid...and when you'll be paid!

Wouldn't it be awful to spend weeks recording an audiobook and then never get paid for the work? With ACX and other established platforms, they keep funds and distribute them when the work is done. More these systems soon. But if you are independently working for someone, as a freelance narrator and producer, here is what I suggest.

You need to know if the author or publisher are prepared to sign an agreement that includes payments and delivery dates, as well as details of rights assigned, and any royalty arrangements.

Also you need, as the narrator, the "clean" version of the whole manuscript. The author needs to understand that an audiobook can't just be recorded with the exact text, word-for-word from the physical or Kindle book. An audiobook has – of course - no illustrations and if there are references to these in the text, the text needs to be adapted, ideally by the author so you, the narrator doesn't get it wrong.

The narrator also would not read out the index or the legal publishing page either with ISBN number, and so on. That's why I always send out an adapted and personalised version of the following document, and you're welcome to use it yourself:

NOTE: This following document is intended to be a useful template for voice actors and audiobook narrators and is intended to be sent to the author or publisher of the book you are about to record and produce. You are welcome to adapt it in any way. The document is provided "as is", and we are not responsible for any misunderstandings or legal action taken if you misuse adapting this communication.

Dear (Author's name)
As I'm sure you'll appreciate, any physical or Kindle book needs to be slightly adapted for audiobook recording, as an audiobook listener cannot see any visuals such as photos, graphics or speech marks. Do you wish to create an "audio-friendly" version, or will you let me adapt the manuscript for you with minor adjustments? For example, I will not usually narrate any references to photographs or illustrations; I will not

narrate the index or the dedication page or any of the legal publishing information that is in the printed version of the book. Do you need "About the Author" recorded at the end?

I also notice that the chapters of your book have titles, but no chapter numbers, so I will assign chapter numbers to go with the chapter names to assist the ACX audiobook upload process and to help the user navigate the chapters. Is that OK?

Maybe you wish to go through the whole manuscript and slightly adjust certain scenes for audio use; if so please let me know, and advise when the fully checked audio version of the manuscript will be delivered ready for recording in my studio.

Could you please give me a few sentences about the main speaking characters in the book please? Let me know their approximate age, the type of person they are and any relationships they have with other characters? Let me know any style of voice or accent you have got in mind for any of the characters.

You are welcome to send links for me to hear by other actors on YouTube etc., if it helps.

I would also need to know how to pronounce your character's names and also place names that are not obvious. Please could you kindly send an audio recording saying slowly these names? Many thanks.

(LIST OF ANY UNUSUAL NAMES)

Unless you tell me otherwise, I will record and edit and master the files to the standard ACX technical specifications.

These are as follows: (Insert SPECS if required)

There will be a standard Intro credit and Outro credit file supplied using the official ACX script:
Intro credit: This is (title of book) written by (author) narrated by (narrator).

Outro credit: This has been (Title) written by (Author) narrated by (Narrator) copyright (Year) by (Author / Publisher). Production copyright (year) by (author / publisher)

The technical standard of the files that I will provide, unless you specify anything different will be:
16 bit mp3 audio files 192Kb/sec; 44.1KHz sampling . Normalized to -3dB with light multiband compression. No music or sound effects.

Every file to start with half a second of silence, at the end of each file to end with 3 to 5 seconds of silence.

Please forward the full manuscript when it's finalised and I'll offer my best quote and an agreement about rights and exact delivery dates of the chapters.

However, if you commission me today, I can promise to deliver all recordings by (DATE) at the latest.

I look forward to working with you on this project.

Best wishes (NARRATOR / AUTHOR)

Then there's the actual agreement that needs to be sent to the author, if you're working direct. Don't forget this form or agreement could be generated the other end, by the author, and sent to the narrator and producer, as long as both sides agree, it doesn't matter. Again you're welcome to adapt my version for your own use, and I am not responsible for any omissions that may be relevant for your own position or circumstance, I offer the agreement "as is".:

NOTE: This document is intended to be a useful template for voice actors and audiobook narrators and is intended to be sent to the author or publisher of the book you are about to record and produce. You are welcome to adapt it in any way. The document is provided "as is", and we are not responsible for any misunderstandings or legal action taken if you misuse this communication.

Narrator Agreement and Contract
Between (Narrator / Producer)
And (Author / Publisher)
Project name:
Date:
(Narrator name) is a professional voiceover and is independent, with no exclusive agent or representation of any kind. Contracts and payments shall be made directly with him. He/She is based in (Country) and is not / is at present registered for Value Added Tax (VAT).

(Narrator / Producer name) has sent a recording of a free, no-obligation sample of the project to you. This agreement and contract is for you to agree that you would like him to either:

a) Continue to record the rest of the project in this style.
b) Offer extra editorial and technical direction another sample page will be recorded. This second demo is still free. Third and subsequent sample pages will be charged at $ X US.

If you are not happy with the sample selection, there is no obligation to continue and you can ignore this agreement and contract.
(Narrator) shall render performer's services in connection with this engagement in a cooperative and professional manner to the best of a performer's ability, and subject to producer's direction and control.

The fee for the recording, editing, optimisation (using Adobe Audition) and the sending of the files to you is as follows:

(NUMBER OF WORDS) / 2.4 = (X)

X / 60 / 60 = Y = Amount of hours, the duration of whole audiobook.

Total cost = Y x (Hourly rate) = $Z

4 staged payments are asked for as follows, about a quarter at these stages:

PAYMENT 1 – START OF RECORDING: $Z / 4

PAYMENT 2 – MID POINT OF RECORDING : $Z / 4

PAYMENT 3 – END OF RECORDING: $Z / 4

PAYMENT 4 – AFTER COMPLETION OF RE-RECORDS : $Z / 4

Files shall be delivered by internet file transfer as either wav, aiff or ACX compliant mp3 files. After 14 days, if the master files are required again, an extra fee of $X shall be required.

The fee for this project includes full "buy-out" with no future monies being requested or demanded in the future. The "buy out" includes selling on, downloading, duplicating on flash media, CD and DVD, as well as encoding in software, apps, devices and in public announcement machinery for perpetuity.

With the rights of the voiceover recording given over 100% to the client, (Narrator / Producer) shall not be held liable in any way for any legal action as a result of the content of the material being broadcast or distributed such as the script causing offence or breaching copyright in any way.

The client confirms that they do own the full legal rights over the text material (Narrator / Producer) has been asked to record.

(Narrator / Producer) agrees to complete the project in 3 working days, assuming he has the full and final script. Any re-takes due to errors in the script or in changing style by the client(s) will be charged for again at the normal rate.

Agreed by Author / Publisher
Signed:

Signed:
NARRATOR / PRODUCER

So in an ideal world, the author or publisher will send over to the narrator and / or producer the version of the manuscript ready for audio book recording, a pronunciation guide if required, and details of any characters who have voices in the book.

Also the author receives the first invoice out of four, or whatever has been agreed, and that is paid before the narrator starts to record at their end.

So that's all well and good, but what about when the author has posted auditions on an online platform, how do the payments work then, when you're not working direct?   We'll go through all things ACX.com next!

27
THE AUDIOBOOK INDUSTRY AND ACX

Let's discuss the Audiobook Creation Exchange platform - ACX.com from the point of view of both authors and publishers, and also narrators; and by the way if you want to be both an author AND a narrator, you need two separate ACX accounts. ACX at the time of writing covers the United States, Canada, the United Kingdom, and Ireland. You need to have an address in one of those places and a tax number and a bank account there.

If you are an author, you have various options when you work with ACX. You can post your book there and search for a narrator and producer of your work. You can listen to various samples from narrators who have posted samples on the website, or you can actually put your book up for audition, and ask people to record about 10 to 15 minutes of your book, and you can choose the best voice for your project.

Once you have chosen a narrator, you can choose between exclusive royalty where you will earn 40% of retail sales income on platforms like Audible, Amazon and iTunes and you get exclusive distribution. Or you can choose non-exclusive royalty system, this means that you have the right to distribute your audiobook elsewhere and you earn 25% of retail sales on Audible, Amazon and iTunes.

When it comes to recording the actual audiobook, if you are an author and you don't want to record or produce it yourself, there are two choices here as well. You can either pay your narrator and producer a one-time fee option such as $200 or $300 per finished hour of audio and you collect full royalties.
By the way, that is a rate per finished hour and not the hours that are worked on the project! Or you may want to pay nothing at all, and share your future royalties with the narrator & producer.

Another advantage of working for ACX is that there is a Bounty Referral Program, where you can earn up to $75 each time a new Audible listener becomes a member using the referral link sent from you and you get this bounty money in addition to any royalties earned from the sale of your audiobook.

Now, if you're an author looking to find a narrator or to distribute your audiobook, you don't have to use ACX, there are other aggregators and platforms out there. The main ones are AUTHORS REPUBLIC and FINDAWAY VOICES. FINDAWAY VOICES – which is a sister company to Draft2Digital that is aimed at self-publishing authors, can distribute your audio book to Audible like ACX does, but to a list of other people like Barnes and Noble, Kobo and Apple Books for consumers.... and ALSO via Hoopla and Overdrive, for library distribution.   Also if you want to look for a narrator and producer as well, like with ACX, you can do this on this platform as well.

FINDAWAY VOICES have a feature called Voice Share, where you can share royalties between author and narrator. Also, if your book starts to do very well, you can buy out your option! If you're an author weighing up the options, read the small print of each platform very carefully as some platforms are better for some types of audiobooks than others. Also you may live in a country which ACX does not recognise, so you may not have the option to use acx.com and HAVE to use an aggregator. If you are in a country that ACX can work with, as we said, the United States, Canada, the United Kingdom and Ireland you do need to have a full home address in one of those locations, tax ID, and a bank account in one of those countries that it works with.

So – that's authors covered. What about us narrators? Register on ACX.com and you can audition for a very wide variety of books of all types.
Once you have registered, you'll see via the top-right SEARCH menu the list of various scripts that are open for recording. It'll say "Titles available for audition".

Some offer a payment per completed hour of audio – sometimes referred to as P.F.H. or Per Finished Hour, and you are bought out completely, you don't get another penny even if the audiobook sells millions; and some are 50/50 deals where you record for free – no payment at all - but receive monthly royalties.

If you're thinking of taking a royalty share, and be paid nothing initially for all the work, I think it's really important to see how successful the author is, with the book that you are about to narrate and produce. So if the book is already available on Amazon or Kindle, look up to see how many reviews it has had, look at the star rating, what people are saying about it, the buzz about the book on social media, and ask yourself what your gut feeling is about it.

But of course, a big seller on Kindle or in print version doesn't necessarily mean an audio version would be a success does it? If the book has lots of photos or diagrams in, or books of many quotes, or recipe books and so on, these have been proven not to work that well in an audio format , so it may be best to not go for a royalty profit share here.

If you think that it IS going to be a big seller, then go for the royalties, and I've had books I am still earning royalties monthly that were recorded many years ago and I am earning far more than if I accepted the "buy out" $200 – or whatever - per hour option.   If you're not that certain, then insist on the buyout option where you're paid "per finished hour" and that's it, no royalties.   Whether you are an author, publisher, narrator, or producer, or all four, you can read full details on the websites of ACX and Findaway voices.

So if you decide to do an audition for a fiction or non-fiction book that takes your fancy, do the best you possibly can of course, unfortunately you can't hear anybody else's audition, but only take the time to make a demo for the author, if you're really sure you've got a good chance of getting it.

If it's a subject you're not really into, or a type of book that you don't think you'll enjoy reading if you were a consumer, why put yourself through misery? There should be plenty of other books out there, available for audition that will be right up your street, that you'll enjoy, and what's more, and more importantly, the listener will hear that you are really into the subject as well, so audition for these instead.
Normally the audition script is about 10 to 15 minutes long.

If it's a fiction book, normally there are sections of narration, and also some character work as well. Don't bother too much about getting the characters exactly right, because maybe the author hasn't really thought yet about what voices should be assigned to each of his or her characters, so don't message the author for these details before you start, they just want to hear your audition and your own personal take on what you think the character could sound like.

You would record and edit the file, put some light compression on, and then upload the MP3 file to ACX, with a short message that doesn't include your personal contact details, and then wait. It may be a few weeks or even months before you hear back, so don't be despondent, some audio book projects really are spread over a long time, it's not like TV or radio commercials which are often done on the day!
When you do get an offer of a job through ACX, you have to agree to work with the author or publisher via the ACX website, and give them some realistic time frame of when you are going to deliver the files. You'll get various agreements that you need to click on and the job starts. As you're not working direct, you won't need the "home-made" agreements that I offered to you earlier.

I strongly suggest that you only record the first chapter before getting detailed feedback from the author. They may have loved your audition, but they may have changed their mind a little bit about the style of the narration, or of some of the character voices, so just record chapter one and upload it and ask for feedback , before proceeding with the rest of them. You really don't want to record the whole of the book again, do you?

At the end of the whole process, when all your files have been uploaded, including the commercial sample, the intro credits, the outro credits and so on, you then get paid via ACX, or the project goes into royalties, and you can look out for money paid into your account, usually by PayPal, every month.

But don't forget direct working with authors or publishers. You send them the audio files, that THEY upload themselves to a platform or distributor of their choice. In fact, if there's a book you love, either fiction or factual, if you're sure there's no audio version available, contact the author or publisher, say you're a fan and offer your services. I've been successful quite a few times with this method! There are plenty of independent audio book producers, for example, one of the biggest is BeeAudio, where they take you through a training process of their recording and checking system before offering you projects. In the UK, there is StoryTec where you can join their community of narrators and producers.

Sometimes smaller audiobook companies are set up to just accept the raw recordings from you, completely unedited and their own teams edit. Usually these production companies pay pretty low rates, but they do have to edit your material, and do all the other work related to bringing out and marketing audiobooks, so it is often a fair deal in the end. It may be a good option for you, if all you want to do is sit and read without the task of editing and cleaning up the files afterwards.

28
WHAT MAKES A GREAT AUDIOBOOK NARRATOR?

If you're already an established voice artist, then really you should be able to hit the ground running with audiobooks, however it may be a bit of a shock that you can't complete jobs as quickly! If you're used to recording short scripts such as corporate promos, radio commercials, or any project that can be fully completed in 20 minutes to half an hour before strolling off for a spot of lunch, it's going to be a big change to have endless pages to cope with, and knowing that you'll have to be consistent in all areas of voice delivery for days or even weeks!

Of course if you are a professional with plenty of stamina and you follow the advice that we're giving you, you should be fine, but I think the most difficult thing for someone to come to terms with concerning audiobook narration for the first time, is the temptation to stop the audiobook recording as soon as another – seemingly more "urgent" voice job comes in - or if they simply get distracted by something else. Even the best written book can get a bit tedious to work on at times and to take a break "just to quickly record" that short radio ad that has just arrived in your "in box" looks very tempting! But do you really want to fall behind on your delivery schedule?

As mentioned before, the key thing to do is to develop a strict "Audiobook Mindset". You need to box off part of the day when you are going to do nothing else but audiobook work. Just ring-fence that time period! It shouldn't be that difficult to do for established voice over talents, because when you are being directed by a client live over headphones, you don't look at emails then do you? You don't start doing your accounts or order online groceries do you in a down-the-line session, do you?

You need to develop a mindset of it being "an exam" in a way. Pretend you are back at school or college, sat in a very quiet exam hall where you're not allowed to talk to anyone else or be distracted by anything, so your full concentration is on the task in hand. The other thing is, if you keep on stopping and starting, you may forget where you are, and when you pick up, your voice may change how it was before, so you really have to watch out for that consistency alteration.

So apart from this new discipline, what other skills are needed? You need to be a very good sight reader, and one where you can be flexible. Narration and voiceover is not just reading aloud in "a nice voice". Emotions often need to change as the text progresses, and character voices have to allude to the mood or emotion the person who is speaking is experiencing. For short average voiceover scripts, you can of course stop and start and the final edit could consist of various "takes" cut together.

For audio book narration, you simply won't have time for this. You won't – honestly! People who start out in voiceover narration often think the best way to tackle the project is to read the book all the way through - without recording - at normal speed, underlining emphasis words, or highlighting sections of text in different colours to represent the different moods and emotions, but honestly this will massively increase your workload. The best, fastest and most natural way is to learn to sightread – yes, right "off the page"…not just so you don't trip up on the actual words, but so you can glance ahead and know how your voice is going to have to change.

If you've ever read to a child at bedtime, you wouldn't pre-read or rehearse that night's Peter Rabbit book, or whatever, would you? You'd pick it up, and it's kind of obvious for anyone how lines should be read, and usually, for young children, the more "over the top" the delivery, the better the reaction and enjoyment of the story that you're reading. So, for adult book narration, you need to train yourself to sightread in a similar manner, glancing ahead so you'll know how your narration style and emotion should change relating to the content and situation. Should your voice be poignant….angry…reflective….menacing…you get my drift. Your sightreading should also instruct your brain to adapt your voice for volume, pace, tone, knowing where to pause. It sounds a lot to do, but it's perfectly possible; if WE can train ourselves, you can as well! You do this by practice; read aloud as much as you can. If you're a complete beginner, you can read aloud to yourself, or volunteer in your community to read stories at a play group, an old folks home, or you can volunteer to record talking newspapers for the visually impaired.

29

AUDIOBOOK NARRATION
PREPARATION

Before any narrator takes on a new project, it's important to look at the whole audiobook text as provided from the author, or publisher. You may have passed an audition using only a small part of the total text, but you need to see everything, the whole manuscript, to make sure that the rest of the book is written to a similar standard and doesn't have later chapters with very hard-to-read or difficult terms, or new characters that would be difficult to bring to life.

Once you have the full manuscript, make sure you insist on getting the Microsoft Word version of it, and not a locked PDF file. This is so you can easily change the font for your recording booth so you can change it to a size and style of font that you personally find easy to read. Also you may want to separate paragraphs more, or to put in notes to yourself in brackets after you have gone through the book. By the way, when it comes to font size, don't think that a larger font makes it easier to read. As long as your eyesight is OK or you have the correct eyewear, go as SMALL as you can on the screen and this way you will reduce mouse scrolling, and your eyes will have less far to scan ahead. A good tip – try it, for all types of voice script!

So once you have the full manuscript, do you have to read it all? You can if you wish to, but to be honest you don't need to read every word. You can skim read and you can train your mind to look out for difficult words or passages. If it was a physical book, it should take you about 30 seconds at most to skim-read each page. For a full screen page of text, about a minute. Make a note of the page numbers that you have concerns about. Then, before recording, you would write to the author or publisher and ask how certain words or names are pronounced or that you don't understand a certain paragraph or any other concerns you have.

You just need to scan the manuscript as a professional, not "to enjoy it" as a reader would, so that any issues do not surprise you in the recording session. If you have to stop recording to ask a question to the author, this will really mess up your workflow big-time.

Professional authors should create different versions of their work for audio recording. For example, many factual books have graphs and photographs that are referred to in the text of the book, which would make absolutely no sense in an audio book version would it? So these would need to be removed. We sometimes get sent "refer to the diagram" and so on in factual scripts, and these will have to be taken out.

This is why it is important to get the whole manuscript. If the author asks you to make up your own mind as to what goes in and stays, or refuses to send you anything other than a PDF file that you cannot easily adapt even with Adobe Acrobat, and what's more they don't want to pay you more to adapt the script, then usually it's best to walk away from the project, because it sounds like the author will be high maintenance, they do not understand your needs, and you'll end up spending much more time in edit when the author doesn't agree with any changes you have made. Basically, what we are saying is that the author or publisher must completely sign up to helping produce the audiobook version and make it very clear to you what is to be read and what is not to be read.

Here are some other questions to ask the author. Do they really want the acknowledgements or the reference sources read by the narrator? What about all the various dedication's, or quotes that you sometimes get on flysheets of books. Surely, they don't want the whole index and page numbers recorded?!

In factual or non-fiction, quite often authors use a term to describe something that's been explained or mentioned before and they use the rather old-fashioned "as discussed above". Well, "above" would be in a textbook, but it's sort of "before" in an audiobook isn't it? But do you need this at all? So all these things need to be changed in the script before recording anything .

But where things get much more confusing, is when there are people talking to each other. In fiction audiobooks, we often see situations on manuscripts where people are talking to each other but unless you can see the speech marks, it's confusing for the listener to know who exactly is saying what line and to whom! Quite often the author won't say "…. John said", or "Steve replied", because it gets a bit tedious after a while.

So in a pretty long conversation, you will just get set a person's piece of speech followed by the other person's piece of speech with just speech marks around them. That's OK if you can see the speech marks, but if you can't, as a listener can't in an audiobook, the author will need to tell you what they want to do in a situation like that.

If the author is not around anymore to tell you, then you've got to take things into your own hands! If there are two people talking to each other this is where your character voices really have to be well distinguished apart. In some books it's quite easy. For example, if you're recording a Bertie Wooster book from the 1920's, a jaunty "Stephen Fry" style narration would be fine for Bertie, and the butler, Jeeves would be a posh, deep British respectful tone. The author, PG Wodehouse, often used the device of one character's line followed by the other character in a conversation; but the poor audio listener can't see the speech marks. So you need to make it clear in your narration.

I put all this to Jeeves:

"Odd, his coming to me. Still, if he did, he did. No argument about that. It must have been a nasty jar for the poor perisher when he found I wasn't here."

"No, sir. Mr. Fink-Nottle did not call to see you, sir."

"Pull yourself together, Jeeves. You've just told me that this is what he has been doing, and assiduously, at that."

"It was I with whom he was desirous of establishing communication, sir."

"You? But I didn't know you had ever met him."

"I had not had that pleasure until he called here, sir. But it appears that Mr. Sipperley, a fellow student of whom Mr. Fink-Nottle had been at the university, recommended him to place his affairs in my hands."

The mystery had conked. I saw all. As I dare say you know, Jeeves's reputation as a counsellor has long been established among the cognoscenti, and the first move of any of my little circle on discovering themselves in any form of soup is always to roll round and put the thing up to him.

So if you had not seen the speech marks, would it have been obvious to a listener who is actually saying what line? Either Bertie the narrator or Bertie talking to Jeeves? Or just Jeeves? It's a trickier book to turn into audio form that you'd think, and PG Wodehouse is not around to help me adapt it into a good audio format. So, the subtlety of your voice has to do all the work.

For this actual job, the Bertie Wooster narration I did closer to the mike, and then for when Bertie was in the conversation, I pulled my head away from the microphone as if I was the other side of the room having my discourse with Jeeves. Then you've just got to keep Bertie "jaunty" and Jeeves in his British butler-style, almost bored timbre!   Of course, with two characters that are wildly different it is fairly straight forward, but things get more complicated when you have two or three people talking together who have similar voice styles and all accents. You can of course, make one character speak a little slower than the others, and one with a type of emotion that is unique to them, remember the "Character Voice Control Panel"?

So what about pictures and photographs? I have worked with some authors who actually want me to mention about pictures, graphs and photographs in the text version of the book. Cleverly, or maybe not, they've figured that if listeners have enjoyed the audio version of the book, they may want to buy the text version as well as a reference, where you can get all the pictures and graphs and visuals that have been mentioned. Of course in the audio version of the book, it gets a bit tedious to not say "have a look at the photograph on page 23" and replace it with "on page 23 of the text version of this audiobook..." so that's another conversation with you and the author.

30
FACTUAL AUDIOBOOK NARRATION

So what sort of narration voice should be used for your audiobook? With a factual, non-fiction book, as always, you need to try and imagine the type of person who would be listening. Remember, that you are just speaking to one person, who is listening intently to you. So, imagine the ideal person who would be listening to it; the person who bought that factual audiobook, because they are really very keen to learn more about the subject matter. Imagine that person, imagine how they are reacting to your words. It is really important to try and target your ideal listener, and you will then structure the whole of your performance to that person, even if they are imaginary.

One of my many audiobooks was about the history of the Berlin Airlift – the rescue deliveries for the people of Berlin when the soviets stopped supplies. So here, it helped that I knew the basics of the story from learning history and I assumed the person listening to the audiobook would already be an avid watcher of historical factual programmes on TV, so a standard BBC style documentary was perfect for this.

Another factual audiobook one was about Forex trading, here it needed to be much more upbeat and modern as the book had plenty of facts and information for the listener to put into action. You needed to image a keen person who just wanted the facts in an enthusiastic manner to get started trading.

Many audiobooks are educational of course; at the time of recording, I've just completed three very long instructional audiobooks for people who are training to be licenced insurance agents. Also recently, I voiced a very academic and detailed audiobook about blockchain technology. For any educational work, you need to be very clear about the facts and information to be emphasised and to slow down over important areas, and the use of pauses to let information sink in is very important.

A trick that many voice talents use when imparting information, whether it's in a documentary, or in a training video is that you need to sound like you are a real expert on the subject matter, when quite often you aren't, and almost certainly you hadn't written the script yourself. So you can try and understand the subject matter, but often it's so complicated and very specialised, so it's almost impossible to fully understand it . Me – an "expert" in blockchain? I think not!

The technique is to emphasise what seemed to be the obvious words, to make you sound like you're the expert. The problem is, and this especially happens with long form audio, when you're narrating a very long factual audio book, you get into a system of emphasising most adjective's on autopilot, and you can make some terrible mistakes if you're not careful.

So with non-fiction, factual books, are there character voices? Sometimes, when there are quotes from people.
Quite often, by the way, you may have to reverse the name attribution to make better sense. You may have a quote from a politician or soldier, or whatever, and in the written version of the book you have the quote printed before the name of the person who said the quote is printed below it. That's fine for a book, as we all scan the author of the quote at the bottom before we read a quote, don't we? In the world of audio, we can't do this!

For an audiobook, you need to put it the other way round, particularly if it's a long quote. So instead of a long quote and then at the end you say that's what Oscar Wilde said, or whatever, you would change it around so that you'd say Oscar Wilde once said, and then say the actual quote.

31
FICTION AUDIOBOOK NARRATION

With a fiction audiobook, you need to take a totally different approach to factual books, as it's usually not just one voice that you have to perform. As well as playing the part of the narrator, in usually your "normal" voice, each of the characters needs to have a unique type of voice. Of course, to the listener, they know it's really just you speaking, no actors just pop in to say these lines, it's not a radio play, but you just need to give a nod to the unique character of each person who is speaking.

So if you're a male voice-over, when a female is speaking, you may want to raise the pitch a bit, clip the voice, and find a suitable pre-set using our "Character Control Panel" mentioned earlier. For other characters, the author may give you specific guidance, and even send you links to YouTube videos they want you to emulate; but, as we've mentioned before, they've got to sound different from each other.

So, one person may sound sort of vaguely bored all the time, one person is generally perky and enthusiastic, someone is sarcastic, one person has a northern accent, one person speaks very slowly, one person may be hyperactive, you get the drift. So how do you assign voices to the characters, and how do you know how many characters there are? That is why, unless your author has kindly provided this information, you need to speed-read the whole manuscript.

Flick through it and write down a list of all the characters who are going to speak. If you don't do this, and just start at the very beginning and put a lot of effort into that first chapter and the initial characters, and give them your best voices, how would you know that that first person you've just given your best voice to, is not killed off in chapter 2?!

Also you may find that if you can only do one Cockney accent for example, there are three other characters that need a Cockney accent that come in the second half, and somehow they've got to sound slightly different from each other!

So ideally you would record a little clip of each of the voices before you even start recording the main narration, and keep the audio sample files stored with their name, so you can be reminded of the sound of the voice every time you come to it. After a few chapters, you may not need to refer to the sample files, but it's important to do this.

The visual element is also important here. If the author has given you any pictures or drawings of the characters – maybe book cover artwork, then pin it up in your studio. For a similar kind of work, voice acting for video games, you're often given 3D mock-up's of each character to get a feel of how the character will look on screen with your voice!

For example, I've recorded the whole series of Ram W. Tuli's excellent comedy thriller spoof books that start with "Dying Horribly At Harding Hall". They are really entertaining, and you'll never guess who did all the murders – look them up on Amazon, I do recommend them!   And these audio books have 1920's style pictures that show the characters and various scenes, so this helps us voiceovers too.

So look through your book and assign a different voice to every character, then record a library of voice samples that you refer to every time the character pops up in the story.

32
CORRECTING NARRATION MISTAKES

If you were giving a live reading in front of a live audience, if you make a mistake, or cough, you would carry on of course. I'm sure even the great Charles Dickens in Victorian times had to stop and have a slurp of water at some point when he was reading his novels out in front of enthralled theatre audiences.

Of course, in an audiobook, or any of our voice recordings, people are paying for perfection. Hopefully you would be monitoring what you are saying using my techniques and thus recording very carefully. So, when you slur a word, or stumble over something, or you hit your microphone, or anything else, you will need to re-record that section.

There are two schools of thought as to how you repair something in a long script if you make a mistake. The first school of thought in my opinion is the wrong school of thought. It's called "punch and roll". Basically, in this system, once you make a mistake, you wind back the recording and play back. As soon as you hear that you come to the point just before the mistake, you "punch in" to record again. You start speaking again immediately and you continue.

I think "punch and roll" is a crazy idea and takes up far more time than the system that I use which is simply when you make a mistake, you leave a reasonably long gap that you can easily see on the audio waveform later.

The thing is, after you have "punched in" and started recording again, how do you know if it was a clean edit or if it sounded natural? Using the punch and roll system, how on earth do you know if you haven't left two breaths in, or clipped a word, or if the intonation from one part of recording to the other matched?

So MY school of thought is, when you make a mistake, stop. Quietly think about why you went wrong by looking at the script in front of you again. Take a sip of water, take a few deep breaths, stretch a bit.

If you need to, just for five to ten seconds, close your eyes and go to your happy place! You won't believe how refreshing doing this can be, in the middle of a long audio book recording. Then, open your eyes and simply repeat the last section where you can easily edit in later.

You'd generally pick up at the start of a sentence or even a complete paragraph, it really depends where you are in the text. Make sure that you do leave a good gap that you'll be able to see in the audio waveform later though. It can be very tempting when you've made a mistake, just to "tut" a bit and then carry on. But you won't be able to see this gap clearly, and the mistake will be left in! Leave a good five to ten second gap so you can identify the mistake area later.

You WILL need to read the whole sentence before a slip-up. If you trip just on a word, you cannot just re-record that word and hope to edit it in - it will sound very unnatural!   Now I do say you can do anything you like when you make a mistake because you're gonna cut the rubbish out anyway, but a very important tip is that you should never swear in front of the microphone.

I know one voice over who actually didn't like his particular client very well and ranted at the microphone about the client an awful lot during his own mistakes, and guess what, yes, he edited out all the swearing and saved it, but unfortunately sent the wrong file – the whole original unedited file got sent to the client. So that was a bit embarrassing wasn't it? So, the number one rule is never swear in front of any microphone, even if you think it's switched off!

One other tip that might be useful to you is that when you are picking up when you've made a mistake, to beforehand explain something to yourself - or to your editor if you're not editing yourself - why you're picking up and where you're picking up from... any little notes like that are useful.

But do them in a really soft voice, and not your normal presenting voice, so the waveform will look like it's a mistake and not part of the finished audio book that would be at normal volume.
With any long script, watch the "fatigue factor".

After a few hours in the voice booth, there is such a big temptation just to get into the rhythm and almost singsong delivery of everything you've done before, you are reading on "remote control" – and a part of your mind wanders to thinking what you are having for dinner tonight - and your eyes don't quite get the right words. And you say the wrong words, but your ear doesn't pick this up, simply because the sound and rhythm are the same as previous sections of recording. So the ear thinks that all is well, but it's not!

It's difficult to describe how this happens, but I've been picked up by clients where they reveal on playback that I said completely the wrong word. I thought that I recorded the one that was in the script, but because the word that I substituted had the same first two or three characters or the same sort of ending, my brain was fooled, and I didn't check, just because I was a little tired....I'd say association when it should be alleviation... or pronounce "graduate" as if it were a noun when I should have said it as a verb like "graduATE". You may say "genetically" when the script said "generically"....or "assessed" when it should have be "accessed". Do you see what I mean?

That's why it's important to take breaks and maybe do another project and come back to it later - don't do more than two hours recording of a long project at a stretch, and that's of course splitting it up into 20 minutes sections.

It's usually the emphasis words that snookers a tired audiobook narrator, especially when you're recording a non-fiction or a factual book, where if you put the wrong emphasis on a word in a sentence or a phrase, the full sense or meaning of what you're saying doesn't come across.   If you're a bit tired and reading "on autopilot", you're likely to deliver a word wrongly, like "CONtract" when you should have said "conTRACT" or to emphasise the wrong words so it will simply not make sense to the listener.

So what else can fight fatigue and assist your consistent delivery for the long haul? Physicality! Gestures! I stand and don't sit for long scripts, as I like to "perform" as if I'm on stage. It works for me. Moving around as you speak and doing appropriate gestures will vastly improve your delivery. Before we mention our tips here, though, a word about the scroll wheel. You need to make sure that the scrolling mouse makes the page on the screen go up at the right speed so that your eyes can read it comfortably.   But what hand should you use for the mouse?

As we don't have a third hand, maybe you don't want to invest in foot pedal, although that is an option, we strongly suggest you leave your dominant hand for all the gesticulations, and use your non-dominant hand to do the simple task of running the scroll wheel to make the text go up the screen.

If your right hand is your dominant one, then use your left hand to use the scroll wheel, because you need your dominant hand to almost conduct yourself, to move around in the air and to be physical with the script.

In a way you need to create your own kind of basic sign language. If you really are a sign-er at all, then adapt that, if you really need to, but of course it's only for your own benefit. Nobody can see you. I've used this technique for so many years, and particularly when I have a difficult sentence, usually a long one where I can't take any breath, by moving my hand in a circular horizontal motion just makes the job much easier, as in the hard sentences, or when tired, I turn from a human into a voice machine with the wheel turning and the voice coming out of the mouth automatically! If there is a multi-syllable word that I find hard to crack, like conceptualisation, or evapotranspiration, you can split these words into individual syllables, but they still don't often become easy to actually say at normal speed. But "conduct" yourself with a moving finger and amazingly, these words become easier to pronounce at speed. Some medical experts will say that this is really just distracting your mind- which is so hung up on doing the word properly - by doing something else, and that may be true, but all I know is that this system works for me, so please try it out! Being physical really helps with character voices as well. Maybe one character swaggers around a bit when talking, so you can do this while keeping "on mike" or another always feels pain, so you could grasp one wrist hard with the other hand when you're doing these lines. Remember, nobody can see you and being "physical" can really help a voice performance. Another very important tip for any long-form project. Before you switch your computer off, make a copy on a memory stick or in the cloud , because wouldn't it be terrible if your computer didn't boot up again, or corrupted the files, or someone stole your computer in the night or whatever! So, make a copy of everything at the end of every day just to be on the safe side. Finally, and I don't apologise for repeating this.... remember the listener, and that will help you maintain the perfect pace of narration for any long project. Imagine their face with headphones on, totally absorbed in what you're imparting to them. They're there at a company eagerly learning some technical or business process via your eLearning modules; or they are tourists looking round a massive temple with you explaining the history to them, or you have them totally enthralled with an audiobook. Your speed of narration and leaving the right amount of gaps and pauses will help them get totally immersed. You are the great "storyteller", let your clear, creative, imaginative voice take your listeners by the hand into your world!

33
DEALING WITH FEEDBACK FROM THE CLIENT

Once you've completed the recording of your often-huge manuscript, and at last you've scrolled to the end, it's also a huge relief as well! Most narrators of audiobooks or massive eLearning projects tend to send files chapter-by-chapter as they are completed to the production company or author, but some authors prefer you to send everything at the very end, it depends how busy they are. But one thing is for certain, after some days or weeks, you're going to get some revisions to record! Your heart may sink at pages and pages of little changes that have to be made, but quite often they look worse than they actually are.

But your life can be made much easier if you can communicate with your client beforehand how you want those notes and revisions sent to you. If they simply resend the script with highlighted bits that they want redone, with notes in the column, it's going to be very hard for you to be able to find out where in the actual audio file is the error or revision.

You may also get this scenario – you could have an author who, on hearing your recordings, change their mind over a section and send you a re-written script for that part!

If there are a just a few of these, you would probably not complain, but I know of a fellow voice actor who was sent a completely revised Word file of the whole audiobook with many changes throughout, but the author hadn't marked down EXACTLY where the changes were made. You would have thought that the author would have at least highlighted the new sections or given the page numbers and "in" and "out" words where the new bits were. So there was no way round it but to record the whole 7 hour audiobook again! In that case, the author did pay a little more when they eventually understood how us narrators work, but it shows how important it is to have a good technical relationship to begin with, before you start recording.

So what I've done is to put together a message to send to the client to explain how I want feedback notes, but is written in such a way to show that it will benefit the both of us. You basically need them to give you the timecodes as well as the details of the changes to be made. These changes need to be listed in the order in which they appear, and the time codes are simply the time into each chapter. No matter what system they are playing the file on, it will have a counter in minutes and seconds, for example the feedback list or "notes" could look like this:

Chapter 1
2'17" Sorry I missed spelled the Doctor's name here, it should be Smythe and not Smith.
15'03 Can you please re-record the whole sentence "Alongside the stream – to – "...allowing herself to cry" It just needs to be a bit more poignant and not matter of fact; thank you.
19'22" Please leave another second gap/pause after the sentence ending "...in San Francisco. "
22'20" – Just retake the section where Andy gets angry from "I can't believe" to when he walks away. He really has lost it by now, give it more emotion please.
And so on.

Clients who give you notes like this they are much easier to work on, because you simply go to your editing program and load up the appropriate chapter, and it's easy to find the words you need to re-record by zapping to the right timecode in Adobe Audition or your own editing software, and off you go.

A quick tip is that if you have a list of time codes in one audio file, as soon as you start working on the early ones in the list, the later time codes in the author's revision list may then not be that accurate, especially if you have been asked to take things out or put things in, or you have been asked to speak slower or faster in earlier sections. This will snooker the timings in the list for subsequent edits.

So don't think that the author has given you wrong time codes as you continue, it's just that as you add or take material away, those later timings are going to be simply off. So that's why you need the manuscript document open as well, and to find the part of the file that you are in, simply identify some unusual words that wouldn't be anywhere else in the book, and put them into "find" In Word, and that's where you will identify the correct part of the manuscript which needs the work on.

When making changes, you do not - I repeat do not - edit any compressed MP3 files that you may have sent to your client. You go back to your original, uncompressed, larger master files that would be in a 24 bit .wav or .aiff format. Once you have made your changes to every chapter, then you would recompress, and re-export as a MP3 files if that is what is required. It is possible of course to make changes to MP3 files, but the quality will not be that good, and what about if there were further changes? You'd be doing further changes to another generation of an already highly compressed file where they can be nasty artefacts to your voice or background hiss increased. So always do editing on the original larger .wav or .aiff files, not on the smaller .mp3 files.

Be very careful that when you do re-record, you listen back to the section before the mistake. Read along carefully to your own voice so you get the same kind of tone and speed and energy. Now open up a new file, and record the section that needs to be edited in. Highlight the new section and put it into memory; so it would usually be Control or Command plus the key C. Go back to the original recording and paste the new section in, and tidy it up. Now go back a good 10 seconds and play to ensure that it isn't obvious that you have rerecorded something and pasted it in. Control or Command plus the key V.

Once you have sent the revised MP3 files to the author or publisher, there may be a few other notes before the whole thing is finished, but let's assume that everything is absolutely fine. So now you've got to "master" the files, go through them all and make sure they are technically perfect so they don't get rejected by ACX or whoever is actually distributing the audio book files to the world. We'll be doing that in the next section "mastering and exporting".

34
MASTERING AND EXPORTING AUDIOBOOKS

All audiobook producers worth their salt have strict technical parameters, so make sure you stick to these unless you want your work rejected! For example, with ACX / Amazon / Audible projects, and also Findaway Voices, they have many very strict technical rules and your files will be rejected if you don't adhere to them. But they are not being nasty just for the sake of it, actually they are on our side as human narrators, because they reject audio books that are created by computer and A.I.! Hurrah!

Generally, if you get it right for ACX specifications, then almost certainly your files will be accepted by other publishers around the world. So let's take a look at all their rules and how we can practically sort them out.

To help with the encoding process with their system, and also to psychologically let the listener know they are at the beginning or end of a chapter, you must have 0.5 seconds of what they call "room tone", but is effectively "silence" at the head of every file, and 1 to 5 seconds at the end.

Now what about the levels? When you sent the files to the author, as long as they could hear them clearly, they're not going to care about technical things like levels, but they will care a lot when your files are rejected because the levels are wrong.

You must normalise to -3dB...not the full 100% you may normalise to usually for your demos so they sound "louder"! Normalizing to -3dB gives Amazon's dubbing system some headroom. Put simply, all files must fall within a specific volume range. By keeping all files within this range - not too loud and not too soft - listeners won't have to constantly adjust the volume of their playback device. Your noise floor should be at least -60dB too for ACX. To check your own noise floor simply, set up normal audio input levels, then just put your audio software program into record and don't talk! If the level meter wavers below -60dB, you'll be fine.

So what sort of files do they want each chapter exported in? They don't want the big WAV files – no - they want MP3's but they have to be a certain type. No matter what kind of software you have, when you export, there will be a dialogue box where you can choose the exact specifications that ACX want for mastered audiobook files.

The files have to be at a data rate of 192kbps or higher MP3, Constant Bit Rate (CBR) at 44.1 kHz. NOT 48KHz! Before going on sale, titles are encoded in a variety of formats that customers have the option of downloading. So 192kbps (or higher), Constant Bit Rate MP3 files are required so this encoding process works without error. You may upload 256kbps or 320kbps files if you'd like, but the difference in quality heard by listeners will be negligible and they make for bigger files for no real gain.

So, do you export them and just send them off? Well, not quite, let's have a look at the other specifications that could get your files rejected, and a lot of them are down to your initial setup of your studio and your recording environment. Let's take a look at this right now.

ACX say that our submitted audiobooks must be consistent in overall sound and formatting. They say "Consistency in audio levels, tone, noise level, spacing, and pronunciation gives the listener an enjoyable experience. Drastic changes can be jarring to the listener and are not reflective of a professional production. " Now the way to do that is if you follow our advice do everything at the same time everyday, and also do it with the same microphone in the same recording facility as well you just need to get into the zone everyday so that you get consistency in the whole recording situation. If you get a head cold half way through the project, you'll have to wait until the cold is over.

As well as providing all the chapters you do also need to provide separate files for the credits both the opening credits and the closing credits and there are certain things that you have to say. At minimum, the opening credits must note the name of the audiobook, the name of the author(s), and the name of the narrator(s). Closing credits must, at minimum, state "the end".

As well as the credit files, you do also need to create an "audio sample" or sometimes called the "commercial sample". This is the file that you hear when you click on the "listen" button on the Amazon website. It needs to be between one and five minutes long, and it should start with narration, not any opening credits or music. It's basically going to offer customers a preview of the audio book, and it's not up to the narrator to choose it, it's best for the author to choose the selection that should be the "commercial sample". The author will know to select an intriguing part from their factual book, or in a fiction book, something that shows the flavour of the story, but doesn't actually give away any of the plot or spoilers.

Just to make it clear, you need to provide:
The OPENING CREDITS file
The CLOSING CREDITS file

ALL THE SEPARATE CHAPTERS, in separate files, all numbered and named correctly

And THE COMMERCIAL SAMPLE – the file that people can hear on the Amazon and Audible website when they're interested in buying the audiobook.

Back to the technical specifications - ACX and most other audio book producers insist on having either mono or stereo files but really would strongly suggest you use mono files , simply because they are smaller and there is less probability of them creating errors when it comes to phase issues or encoding. So make sure everything is just in good old Mono. Us narrators have only one mouth.

Each file that you upload as well as being in mono and being in the technical specifications that we've talked about, should never be longer than 120 minutes.

This is because of the technical system that's used for uploading and downloading. If the author has given you a huge, long chapter that actually turned out longer than 120 minutes, you will have to split it into two or three, and a secondary section header must be included on continuations.

35
SURVIVING DIRECTED SESSIONS

If you're a voice over with your own home studio, you'll know there are two ways you can record and edit jobs, the first is to simply get all the instructions and the script from the client. You fulfil those instructions and send them a take or a couple of takes, whatever is agreed to them and wait for feedback. That feedback may mean that you have to record again.

If you have a fussy client, or one that doesn't really knows what they want, then quite often it's best to insist on a directed session. This means that you have your headphones on in the booth, and they talk to you over the headphones and that way they hopefully get exactly the take they want.

It can be done via one of the domestic audio connection systems, like Zoom or Skype, but more likely you will get a link for one of the internet systems where the client can hear your voice at a far better quality. There are many of these systems, such as ipDTL, Cleanfeed, Session Link Pro, Whereby, and Bodalgo Call.

Most of these systems need all users to have the Chrome browser installed, and they are all much of a muchness, apart from one I haven't mentioned yet called Source Connect and Source Connect Pro. Both these systems have a slightly superior way of working where the audio feed isn't stretched out if a connection is lost for a short spell, so the audio they get to hear in their studio is more of a true representation of your performance. This is why quite often you see auditions that say *"only available to voice artists if you have Source Connect or Source Connect Pro"*. By the way, Source Connect Now doesn't count, it's the budget variety of the connection system!

No matter what system they connect to you to monitor, you always have to record locally at your end anyway to be sure, and usually the studio always asks for you to send them the actual unedited files recorded at your end to them. That way they get the best quality recording from you.

Some voice overs charge extra for directed sessions, which is strange in a way, because quite often a directed session makes your life easier. You'll know that a job is done and dusted after you've finished it and you've sent it off, because you've actually heard the voice of the producer saying *"yes that's exactly what we want, no problem!"* So they are extremely unlikely that they'll come back again for some retakes.

When you are recording without any feedback in your studio at all, there is a high likelihood that you haven't got it quite right. So, I personally would not charge extra for a directed session, because in many circumstances, it takes you less time to do overall and is less hassle, as you've got the client actually listening to you and giving you feedback as if he or she was in the same studio as you.
The other advantage of having a live directed session, is that you can create a personal relationship. You can have a nice chat with the engineers in the studio, the producer, and even the end client who may be on the session somewhere.

So you can wow them all with your personality and hopefully they'll remember you fondly to book you for another session next time. So, a directed session gives you an opportunity for your personality to shine through, whereas it wouldn't do this so much if you have just self-directed yourself and emailed a download link without even talking to anyone. So I would say, if a client is prepared to self-direct, grab it with both hands, and don't charge them extra for it.

However, sometimes you get very difficult sessions, where you have multiple people all shouting in your ear at once, and quite often in different languages and accents, and it can get a bit, shall we say, distressing sometimes! If you've ever seen the Bill Murray film *"Lost In Translation"*, you'll know what I mean by this! I recently had a session directed from three different cities in Italy, one was where the production company was based, one was the home of the advertising agency, and one was where the client was based. And there were two people at each location! So there were in total six people listening to my takes, and commenting on them into my headphones.

However quite often they gave up speaking in English then went into full speed Italian which I don't unfortunately understand! So, after a couple of minutes of them all arguing with each other over my last take, I then wait to hear one of them break back into English, and tell me what to do next! All very amusing. We got exactly what they wanted in the end.

Next, I want to give my advice on something that could happen in a external studio as well as directed over your headphones at home. Quite often, you're often asked for a few more takes. They say *"Let's just try it again"*. And if you ask what was wrong with the last take, quite often you won't get an answer. Either they're not sure how to express what is wrong with your last take, or they want to justify their job and spin out the hour-long studio hire.

Mostly in my experience, I found that I was dealing with inexperienced people who simply haven't worked with many voice artists before, so if you get in this situation, you need to subtly and tactfully "teach" them the ropes. I've had directors who have OK'd a take that was pretty terrible, and it was ME that had to insist on our doing it again. This sort of situation takes the *"Words to the Wise"* adage to a new level!

So what do you do when you're asked for *"one more take"*? Well, there's no point in just doing exactly what you did last time. So, you'd simply experiment with different techniques. Make sure you have fully interpreted the script and got the *"emphasis words"* right as well and consider the FIVE VOCAL ELEMENTS if it's appropriate. Have fun with it - tweak the emotion with the script, work with more irony, pathos or whatever. See what happens. Use some dramatic pauses.

Sometimes just very, very subtly, stretching some words quite often makes this script sound different. Try varying the speed of your read in factual and training scripts. This often works very well. So, you go quite fast over the obvious ones that many listeners could know already. But slow down over the new material. Or try smiling. In the stress of a recording situation, voice artists forget to smile and even if it's not a "funny" script, it may well be a positive script and just smiling while speaking can really help in making the whole read come alive.

Let me tell you about another type of experience I've had fairly regularly when I've had inexperienced directors talking in my headphones. When you're recording a TV or radio commercial, every split-second counts of course. I've had the experience where the director has got the script and a stopwatch at their end, and they've already got a rough version of the commercial with a computer voice that fills the exact VO slot of 26 seconds.

Now the computer doesn't have to breathe does it? When I do my recording in the live session, of course I do have to breathe a few times! These can easily be chopped out in edit, but I still have to breathe during the recording. So I remember one particular session where I gave some excellent takes, but the takes were about a second over the 26 second limit. If the breaths were taken out it would certainly take the recording to the exact time, but the client wasn't having it. He wanted a proper recording, that was exactly 26 seconds.

A part of me wanted to say "hang on though, surely you can cut the breaths out afterwards, can't you?". But in this particular session I didn't say that, because he was pretty full of his own importance, and I didn't really want to upset him. So, in the end I just had to keep going and record faster reads that weren't necessarily as good as the other reads.   In the end they accepted a faster read that was far inferior, and they left the nasty breaths in! Sigh....

For the other sessions that this is happened in, I managed to subtly say something like *"Look, just hang on a second, I'll just cut out the breaths at my end and will check the time then and send it to you"*, and that's the nice situation where everybody wins. They'll appreciate your expertise in training them as to how to deal with voiceovers and directing when time is tight in an advert, and you get the satisfaction of knowing that they have taken your best take. So I hope you don't feel daunted by being directed in the studio or via the internet; just try and enjoy the experience and feel free to ask any questions that will help you get a good read. Be honest as well. If they've booked 30 minutes with you and the clock is getting onto about 50 minutes or so, just say that you have another session booked in soon, even if you haven't.

At the end of the day, script interpretation is key to being successful as a voice artist in the booth when you're working with a live director. Look not at the words but the structure, and by doing this, you'll be able to identify the various sections of the script and where you should subtly change your voice style accordingly. Remember the director and their team have been living with this script for quite often many weeks, and you have just come into it almost cold. So you need to get up to speed very quickly so you need to think the same way that they are thinking. Just absorb the message or messages you are conveying, and just come at it from a different angle.

For example, a classic structure of a commercial or a promo script for a product or service is Problem, Solution, Call to Action. Quite often you've got a problem. Here's our solution. Call this number right now. Problem. Solution. Call to Action. A classic structure. So by understanding the structure of the script you've got, particularly with commercials you'll be able to hit the ground running.

So I hope you found these pointers useful for when your director asks you for *"just one more take"*.

Finally a few practical technical tips for directed voice sessions.

1) If you're self-conscious, you don't have to have the camera on if it's a Zoom or Skype session. Just say your camera is not working or you don't have a camera in the booth, or you want to optimise the broadband if they ask why they can't see you.

2) Always have a glass of water in the booth with you and sip between each take.

3) If there is a crazy long sentence in the script and you have difficulty with it, flag this up before you record, as the client or producer may realise that it would be better split into two or something like that.

4) If a long sentence can't be split, explain that you're going to leave a deliberate "breath gap" that will be edited afterwards. This is, as explained before, where you stop mid-sentence, usually at a comma, gasp a big noisy breath and then continue at the same energy level, so when you chop the breath out it will sound natural. Experienced producers will understand what you're doing, but less experienced ones may not.

5) If the client is using a technically inferior system like Zoom, Skype or even a phone patch, make absolutely sure that you are recording at your end. Use my "belts and braces" system of recording both on the computer and a solid-state recorder to be sure.

6) When you are about to send your recording after the session via WeTransfer or some such system, don't bother editing out the mistakes or the gaps between takes. Sometimes the producer will not be counting takes but will know that at 18 minutes into the session, you recorded the best take, so just send the whole recording as an uncompressed 24-bit wav file with all the chat and all the mistakes!

7) Finally don't miss your session time! Check the time zone they are in and when your session is. Just set yourself double alarms and get yourself set up a good 15 minutes beforehand and look at the scripts and understand who you'll be speaking to. Switch off your phone at your end, and connect to their link about 5 minutes to when you are supposed to be there. Always turn up early. That way you should get a nice chat with the studio engineer, before the director arrives, and it shows you're keen and professional.

36
RECORDING AT AN EXTERNAL STUDIO

Now note the title is "External" Studio and not a "Professional" Studio, because your own set up, whether it's at your home or local business centre, should be just as professional in workflow and technical expertise as the swanky shiny recording studios in the city you go to with the smiling receptionist and the free Starbucks on tap. Well, as long as your output material is comparable in quality, there's no need to be jealous of other studios, even though you don't have the luxury of the client's lounge or the cake trolley.

Now, even though most of your work as a voiceover might well be at your own facility and using the Internet to communicate with clients and to send them files around the Earth, there will be occasions when you'll be invited to physically travel to studios. Often these will be for well-paid commercial voiceovers and there'll be good opportunities to meet with, say, ad agency people and even the clients of the product or service being advertised. So it's well worth dropping everything and going to the session, even though, you know, in your heart you could do the job just as well at home being directed by any of the Internet systems like Source Connect.

Now, there are, of course, some situations where you do HAVE to be in the studio with others. What if you have, say, a dialogue part with another voice actor? It's difficult to record and control conversations between two or more actors using the Internet and in different studios with varying quality of microphone, varying acoustics of their voice booths and so on. So you need to be together, although during the pandemic, it has been astonishing the number of really convincing radio dramas that were produced with none of the actors actually having met each other, doing it all via Internet connections from their own booths.

You may also have to be physically at a studio to synchronise "lip-sync" your voice to a film or video and it's not practical via the internet no matter how fast your connection. It's certainly not practical to do "loop dubbing" remotely to a high standard, where you are acting the words of a non-English actor on a film or video. We've all seen really badly dubbed films where the speech does not fit the mouth movements of the actors, and many producers of non-English films that become global hits usually insist on using subtitles rather than dubbing into other languages, as it's so hard to get right as well as the huge extra expense.

With lip-sync work, first of all, the very underappreciated translators have to turn the original language dialogue into English - not just so it makes sense and captures the essence of the character(s), but also so that every type of mouth movement of the actors on screen matches the English words, syllable by syllable. This is very challenging in itself. Then you need to cast voice actors who fit the on-screen characters and every scene needs to fit the acoustic and action on screen. For example, people sound different walking along in an underground carpark having an argument, than cosily chatting on a sofa, don't they? The actual recording process in lip-sync dubbing is to play one line over and over and over again in your headphones watching the screen in front of you, and you record multiple takes and if the engineer can't slide any of your takes a few frames left or right to match the mouth movements of the on-screen actor exactly, then you go through another round. It's hard work.

So for jobs that don't really need to be at a physical city centre studio, like most other VO jobs, why do you have to go there? Quite often, the creative agency people need to justify their jobs and the session provides an opportunity to physically meet up with the end client and other people associated with the project. It also of course provides YOU with a good opportunity to leave a professional positive impression.

So here are the rules of the game. You reply to the studio request promptly and professionally. Confirm the time, date and studio in your email reply. Agencies are often busy and have been known to mix up bookings. Listen to the demo recording you sent to them that actually got you the gig over everyone else that auditioned. Try and understand what they liked about it. Memorize every nuance before you go to the studio. Arrive at the studio a good 20 minutes before you need to. Make some excuse like the train was early or something. You see, even if your agency contact isn't there, it's a good opportunity to schmooze the receptionist or technical people who may have some other work for you in their "in-tray", even if it's just a demo. This tip really pays dividends.

Don't forget to leave your business card when the ad agency person or people arrive. And I say people. I was once in a TV commercial session in London, five agency people and four clients, all to hear a very simple voice over session, say hello and engage with some relevant small talk about the project.

Say some white lies if need be, but to try and make it not about the weather or about your holidays or about the tie you admire or anything, but something about the product or something about the script or its humour or what a great idea or something like that. Keep the chat on "work" and you never know, you could be just right for another project the agency have soon.

Next tip, do NOT adjust the microphone in the booth. It's bad enough the studio owner and technicians knowing that their livelihoods is being eroded by people like you with your own studios at home, and then you come in and fiddle with their precious Neumann's. When you are in the voice booth, the control room will communicate with you via headphones. Now, you may not wear headphones in your own studio, so if this puts you off, take one side off an ear.

Just like with home directed sessions, you'll often be asked for take after take, so just do as they ask. Try a few variations of voice or delivery. Show your flexibility. Even though they will probably go back and use take one in the end!

Once the best takes been accepted by all, don't outstay your welcome. The ad agency may need to discuss other matters with the client while they have them in the studio. So shake hands, say your farewells, make sure they remember your name.

37
ESSENTIAL EFFICIENCY TECHNIQUES

As we're always being told even from when we were kids, to be efficient and to get things done in this life, you've got to be organised and know where things are. Unfortunately, in our very creative media world, you will know that most creative people just aren't that organised. And so because of that, they aren't efficient either. So this is a problem, isn't it?

If you are hopelessly disorganised, not knowing what jobs are happening where and when, or you can't remember where you put that recording you did last week that the client now desperately wants to hear, this section is for you. You may disagree or completely hate the suggestions I have, but all I know is that they have worked very efficiently for me for many years!

First of all, no doubt you have many drives on your computer. I recommend that you keep your voice over work on only one drive, to save flicking round the drives in your work. On that drive, you would create a folder with simply the name of the year.... because it's a number, it will always be towards the top of the alphabetical list and easy to find! Then in every year folder, you would create a separate folder for each month.

So everything voice-related would go in there, for the relevant month. I did experiment with having separate folders for demos and for real jobs, but there were many occasions where a demo actually became a real job, and often they used the actual demo recording, so it will save you an awful lot of time if you put everything from the month in the correct folder. This will help you as well, when you are trying to find a job from months ago, a long-forgotten project that is being revived, and the client wants you to replicate the voice style of something you just can't remember now. In your email program, you would find the chain of messages from the last job, and from that you will get the date, and from that, you'd know the folder where those pesky files are going to be.

So you have a folder for each month, and jobs and auditions go in there. Don't make sub folders for demos or auditions. But, I DO make sub folders for really big jobs that happen in that month, like eLearning, audio books, tourism guides, things that usually take a couple of days at least to do. Because here you can keep in one folder the script or scripts, the pronunciation guides, the WAV files , and the MP3 files as well all in separate folders in this one folder for the whole big job.

But generally, for individual one-off jobs, I just keep them all in the month folder. It's really important to name the files after something you can easily find afterwards. I know what it's like when you're crazy busy, and you're in a bad mood, and you've just read the audition script, and it doesn't give any idea of what the script is really about. But don't just type "demo_your name.mp3. There must be some handle on it, and even if you're doing a demo for a website like Voices.com, they would have called it something, so type exactly that even if it's something vague like "Corporate Video" then you'd type exactly that then an underscore, then the word Demo, then you'd type another underscore then your name.mp3 as the file name. If you did need to find the original demo again for something you auditioned for on a voice over website, the site would have a date anyway, so it's even more important to keep things in month order.

Some voice overs I know have a weekly folder, and having 52 folders over a year may seem like a good idea to people who have a high turnover of jobs, but for me and the types of clients I have, when does the week start? Is it a European or American week, or a Middle Eastern week?!   For me, the month system works fine.

Now, if you looked through my Explorer or Finder, through my voice over files, you may wonder why there are two versions of each WAV file. Well, if you have taken any of my **Voiceovermasterclass.com** courses, you'll know that I am a big fan of always keeping the original UN-processed files. Indeed, many clients absolutely insist on being sent this option, with no processing at all - no noise gating, no compression no EQ, and so on.

However, for the types of jobs I usually do, and you may be the same, it's very rarely that this happens, and it's usually only very high-end jobs, where there is a budget to do the full voiceover processing work at the studio end. Most of my clients are of a type where they appreciate that I have not just edited the voice over recording, to get rid of mistakes and even breaths if appropriate, but also that I have processed it to sound its best.

As I'm lucky enough to have a really good voice booth, I don't need a noise gate to get rid of any low-level background noise, and my microphone is excellent, so I don't need to add any equalisation curve to the file, but what I do add is compression, and I am a fan of Adobe Audition's multiband compressor, and I use a tweaked version of their "Broadcast" pre-set. This makes my recording sound much richer, more powerful, and just clearer for the listener, especially if music is going to be mixed with it. In fact, for really over-the-top shouty work I do, like for example for the Epic Economist channel on YouTube, I double compress it, because that's the style that they want, crazy punchy all the time with no extreme highs and lows.

For new clients, you don't really want to ask them every time if they want compressed or non-compressed files, because this may confuse them if they're not technical, or they may not even understand what you are talking about. They just want a voice over file that sounds good. Don't complicate the issue!

So the system I have for absolutely everything I do, is to always keep 2 copies of the edited WAV file. After finishing editing the file, I save the file, and then add the compression, and then I "Save AS" exactly the same title of the file, but with a subtle underscore before my name.

This is the actual file that I send via a WeTransfer link to the client, who has absolutely no idea that there is another file that is completely UN processed they never got. However if they do insist on having the original raw file to process themselves, I have got it , and I can easily find it. Of course, if there are any changes to be made to the project, you'd always return to the uncompressed raw file, and once complete you'd re-process and save it as a Version 2 - "V2".

JOB LISTING AND INVOICING EFFICIENCY

Wouldn't it be awful if you did a voiceover job, and then you had kind of forgotten about it because other ones came in, and you forgot to invoice for it? So here are my suggested methods for never forgetting anything that you've done and for invoicing efficiently.

Now you may want to do all this electronically – but call me old fashioned - I use clipboards in my studio. One clipboard is for jobs, one clipboard is for marketing and potential jobs. Let's start with the jobs, shall we?

I have a clipboard with sheets of paper on it from a template that I simply created in Word. It basically has the columns of date, script name, client, fee, and an extra column at the end which I tick when I've actually invoiced the client. Now, you only use this clipboard when there is a job that isn't going to be stored anywhere else. For example, I have some regular jobs at a fixed fee that get invoiced monthly, so there's no point putting those on the sheet. Also, jobs that you get via websites such as Voice Realm, Voices.com, VO

Planet, Voiceovers.com, Fiverr, Voiver.com, Voice Jungle, and Envato Studios and so on, all those details of the job, script, feedback, payments and so on, are actually stored on the website and you get paid from the website, so again, there's no point making a separate list of those jobs.

But of course, not all voice over websites have a system like this. For example, there are loads of directory voice over sites that simply put you in touch with a client, and either the client or you pay for this service. But once you and the client gets together, then you're on your own - it's up to you to be organised. So, if you're registered on the likes of Bodalgo, Speakonline, Voice 123, Mandy.com, these are the types of jobs to put on your sheet to remind you to invoice. You would also put on your list of course direct clients, which maybe, if you're like me, is where the lion's share of where your work comes from.

When I'm asked to give a quote for a job, I put it on the form, in pencil - now that really is old fashioned, isn't it! It turns to ink when it's confirmed.   It's sad when I have to rub a pencilled job out, but that doesn't happen very often thank goodness!

So with a system like this, you know you've got all bases covered. All your online paid jobs are going to be on the various websites, and all the ones where you know you have got to invoice clients direct, are going to be on the clipboard. Nothing can possibly go wrong can it? Well yes it can, if you forget to put it on the sheet! So always have it handy with you, and if you are out and about and accept a job on your phone, make sure you add it on the sheet when you get home.

When it comes to invoicing, as I explain in detail later, don't send the invoice with the actual recording, because that is a) a little bit rude and desperate and b) there may be retakes to do or even an addition to the script for which you will be paid more!

I tend to do invoicing at the weekend, and it's only an hour out of your weekend, but at least it's a set time to do it. Unless you really are desperate for money, I would suggest that the sweet spot for sending your invoice is about three or four weeks after your voice over has been accepted. If you send it earlier than that, then the client may not have been paid by the end client yet, but if you send it at about the same time the client themselves have got paid, you're likely to be paid quicker.

Now what happens if you haven't really heard back from a client after you sent the final files in? All sorts of things can go wrong with a job, and I sometimes think the worst, but usually things turn out absolutely fine, and the reason your client hasn't come back to you, is that they're simply busy and they've forgotten about you. So, after a couple of weeks have gone past in this situation, I would send a friendly email asking if everything is OK with the job, and ask if you can send your invoice in now. This is where I use the final column on the sheet, and put a question mark if I've actually sent an email like this. Now you may be thinking *"well surely I'll remember if I contacted that client won't I?"* But if you have the amount of scripts that I have got in a day and in a week, many of them are for pretty similar jobs, you do tend to forget! If you're not getting that amount of scripts, well, we'll tackle that in the marketing section!

When a client says "send the invoice", that question mark is scrubbed out, and there is a tick in its place. That's when I go over to my invoicing software. Other systems are available, but I use XERO, which is very simple to understand, and safely and securely reads all your bank accounts, so it gives you a reflection of what's in every account, and you can also issue invoices and store receipts as well.

These online systems are really fantastic, because gone are the days where you take along a carrier bag of receipts and scruffy bits of paper to your accountant once every year, and with an online system like this, your accountant can log into your account anytime, and it's very efficient and saves so much time. It's useful as well for seeing how well your business is doing, as you can see your profit and loss charts at a click of a button. If you are perfectly happy with doing things on good ol' Excel sheets, I really would recommend just getting a free trial on one of the systems like XERO as I think you will say goodbye to the old days of Excel. You can also see at a glance which invoices haven't been paid yet, and how many days they are overdue.

I actually use my XERO as a sort of CRM as well, because for every client I have their contact details, and also I can clearly see how much work I have done with them over any kind of time period, so it's extremely useful for marketing purposes.

That's what I use the SECOND clipboard for.

VOICEOVER EDITING EFFICIENCY

What about editing fast?   Now obviously I'm going to mention keyboard shortcuts now, and if you still haven't gotten onto using these yet, you really are wasting a lot of time messing around with menus and things! If you're a professional and you subscribe to Adobe Audition, you should know that if you hold the ALT or OPTION key down and click K up comes the shortcut menu, which you can customize to your hearts delight.

The main keyboard shortcuts I use all the time are 1 for normalisation, 2 for multi band compression, X for silence , F for amplify or reduce sound volume, and Z for De-Clicker for lip-smacks. If you do a lot of ACX Audiobooks, where you want exactly 0.5 seconds of silence at the start of chapters and exactly 3.5 seconds at the end of every chapter, keyboard shortcuts can save so much time here as well.

My mega keyboard shortcut is for quick mastering of audition recordings. Once you have hacked any mistakes out, I just click my M key on my keyboard, and this triggers a recorded "favourite" that consists of normalisation, compression, and also a soft noise gate that I have to use if I'm recording in my demo studio, and then it normalizes again. So one simple keystroke just makes the file ready to send out as a demo.

How to set this up? In Adobe Audition, you click the favourites menu at the top, and then select "start recording favourites". After you go through all the processing you wish, then you click "stop recording favourites", and call it a pre-set. Then this pre-set you will find in the keyboard shortcut menu, (ALT+K) where you can assign it a key by dragging to that key. I assign it the "M" key for "Master" but it's up to you. If there's some shortcut already assigned to any key you want, just delete it and remember to click SAVE when you're done.

38
THE TEN COMMANDMENTS OF CLIENT ETIQUETTE

With every profession, no matter what you are, you will get on in your career if you get on with other people. Most folk in this world are actually pretty reasonable and pleasant, and they want to surround themselves with people just like them. It's sort of obvious really isn't it, if your clients find you to be a little bit of a hustler, greedy, pushy, or just someone who annoyingly doesn't get back to them promptly, they won't want to work with you.

You may think that you are the nicest person on the planet, but because most of our work as voice-overs is now done remotely over the Internet to people you will never physically meet, it's important to stick to these essential etiquette rules. I cannot over emphasise how important all this is if you want your career as a voiceover artist to flourish. People like working with nice people. People like doing business with efficient and responsive people. It's as simple as that.

So here we go with the 10 commandments of voiceover etiquette.

Commandment 1 –
Thou shalt reply straight away. No matter what you doing, always keep an eye out for your emails, texts and what's app notifications, because the more responsive you are to clients, the more positive psychological Brownie points you'll get. And more people will book you to record their voice-overs. Even if you can't actually record their demo or paid scripts straight away, at least reply as soon as you can within minutes, and give them a realistic time when you can. I am sure that I personally get a lot of work, not because I may be the best voiceover for the job, or the cheapest, but because I

always respond quickly, and am generally in the studio on various projects working on something every day. Make yourself available and respond fast.

Commandment 2 –
Thy customer is always right. What I mean by this? Well usually the voiceover artist is at the end of a pretty long chain for most projects, particularly in the corporate and commercial world. The actual boss of the client's company may have asked his communications team to create a corporate video, for example, they then contact an external video production company, who then put the work out to an animation company, who then put out the voiceover work to a voice agency, and then that voice agency finds you. So you're at the end of a very long chain. If you complain about the script, or suggest changes to make it better, thinking you are doing them a favour, you really are not, because the person who wrote the script may be two or three people up this chain. The person who hires you may actually agree with your suggestions, but it would be too embarrassing and not really in etiquette for them to make changes without checking it with the top person, and this creates hassle all round. Just shut up and read the script. If they decide to change it later, and improve it, to maybe just the way you wanted it, that's fine, you get paid again! So just "read the copy, the copy's good".

Commandment 3 –
Thy shalt always go the extra mile. This means that if they asked for a couple of takes, you give them three. If they asked for three takes, you added an extra one for security, or in a completely different style that they may like. However, there are some clients that find different takes annoying, especially those who haven't got English as their first language. They probably won't know the difference between the subtleties of the different takes. So don't embarrass them, and give yourself extra work. If you feel they are someone who isn't fully au fait with the English language and grammar, or subtle accent changes, just do one really good fantastic take, that

you feel would really hit their target audience well, just send them that.   That is commandment three of our etiquette 10.

Commandment 4-
Thy shalt get thy clients names right. Particularly if you have an unusually named client, it is so important not to make yourself look an idiot, and spell their name incorrectly on the email reply or file name you send them. If it's a really long complicated name, that you are not familiar with, simply highlight the name in their email and copy and paste it. It's quite easy, and you won't offend the person at the other end. Simples!

Commandment 5-
Thy shalt make it easy for clients to get your files. Don't let them have to download any new software just so they can access your voiceover files. Don't let them have to register to any weird file transfer system. I personally have used WeTransfer for years, because you simply send the link in the email, and they just download the file to their computer at their end. All very simple, no registration, no downloads, no bugging emails afterwards from the system. I don't personally use Dropbox, or any other system like that, because I personally find it very confusing to navigate, and people just want the file at their end where they know where it is, and where they can work with it, not in some vague place in the cloud where other people may have access.

Commandment 6-
Don't brag. When you are pitching for a job, or you are sending out emails, or phoning up people, don't do the big-headed thing about listing all the big names you have voiced for in the past. You can put this on your website if you like, but in a direct pitch, people just want to know what YOU can do for THEM, and it may even backfire if you state that you have worked for some big-name organisations who are the direct RIVALS to the companies that that particular advertising agency represents. So just be pleasant and concise in your communication, and think about the needs of your client,

without going on about all the big flashy studios in the big cities that you have been booked in. People just care about their own projects, they really do! As long as you come over as professional and competent, and you have the voice they need, you've got the job, it's as simple as that!

Commandment 7 –
Don't be greedy. We are very lucky in this voice-over world, of earning really decent money, for what is actually a pretty easy job. Particularly when you have done it for some years, and you have learnt the skills of the trade, it becomes no big deal to read and record and edit a script, or even an audiobook, almost on autopilot.

So don't be greedy when asking for money in a quote, I know it's strange how exactly the same amount of work in your studio can be paid vastly differently depending on where it is going to be used, but hey, that's the way the voiceover world is set up. Of course, you'd be stupid to say no to the big bucks if they are offered to you, but if the client genuinely sounds like they haven't got a big budget for your services, don't put the phone down on them or call them names for insulting your professionalism offering just $100 for a small and simple non-broadcast script; just do it with a smile, but make it clear that you are doing them a favour, and you would appreciate your full rate next time. They will love you and you will get repeat business. Win Win!

Commandment 8 –
Never send the invoice in straight away. I know voiceovers who send the invoice in exactly the same email as the link to the recording, and that is just plain arrogant and rude. At least wait till they reply and say "hey that's just what we want!" You should know that they quite often won't get the money for the job from the person they are providing your voiceover to as part of their package, for a good month or more, so it's very good etiquette to hold back. Just wait until they are absolutely 100% happy with your voiceover recording, and it has been fully signed off, and only then

send in the invoice. Quite often there are extra lines you are asked to record afterwards, so the invoice may need to be added to, so you are giving yourself extra work if you send in the first invoice with your first recording. Just wait till the job is over, then wait at least a week, then send in the invoice.

Your clients will generally love you for doing this. If you're dealing with a very big agency, where you send your invoice to an anonymous independent finance office, then you don't need to worry about this, because some faceless accountant will simply put your invoice in a folder ready for paying. However, if you are dealing with the actual person who booked you, who may be an independent producer, follow this commandment, and they will love you for ever!

Commandment 9 –
Never, ever add music to custom demos. Yes, you can add music if you like to your showreels on your website, that will give a little bit of atmosphere and extra professionalism to your show reels, but when clients are asking for a custom demo, quite often they already have the video timeline ready, and they simply place in the demos on the video to see if it fits. If they already have carefully chosen music on their video timeline, which is quite often the case, then if you have sent in a demo and added your own music, how can they possibly do this? You will be rejected. It's also a bit of an insult to the producer, as they normally choose the music. How dare you, the voiceover choose a piece of music to put on your custom demo? So just send the audio, lightly compressed but without any music.   Don't waste your time adding music, or any sound effects.

Commandment 10-
Never ever complain when you lose a job. This isn't when you simply put in demos with loads of other people on a voice site and you don't get offered the gig. This is where you think you have a solid booking, but it gets pulled, maybe at the last minute, if you haven't actually recorded anything, just take it on the chin. I know

voice-overs who would send in an invoice, saying they had a firm booking that needs compensation, or they have 24-hour cancellation policy, or some nonsense, and this is just going to get them in the bad books of the client. Just be reasonable and pleasant. Why should you get paid, because the person who booked you may find themselves without payment for their part of this cancelled project as well. So all comes down in the end to just being nice to people, being reasonable, and the world will reward you in plenty.

39
VOICEOVER VACATIONS

The whole point of a vacation, or a holiday as we quaintly say in the British Isles, is just that, to take a break from being in your voice booth all day. However, you may have, like I have, some regular clients, who come to you with regular scripts, and you really don't want to inconvenience them do you? It could be a situation where your client is a production company who have to keep things sweet with their own end-client, so it looks bad when they can't get the exact regular voice the end-client demands. You don't want to go away on holiday, and return to find that they have found someone else who they will continue to use even when you have returned, do you?

This is where the pop-up voice over booth business makes their cash! If you Google "pop up or portable voice over booth", you will find quite a few things that you can buy. But of course, nobody can see you when you're recording, so you don't have to spend a fortune on a custom travel voice booth that's made for this job. It's also something else to take on holiday with you isn't it? So what I do, is just to pack the absolute basics. I take the microphone and pop filter in a big padded bag ,a small stand, an XLR cable, an audio recorder, plus a USB lead, to connect this to my solid-state laptop for editing. Solid state of course, meaning that it's quiet, with no pesky fan ruining the recordings while I'm reading off the screen. You could of course, take the SD card out, and put this in your laptop, it's up to you.

This is the easy part. The hard thing in a hotel room, or in the accommodation where you are staying on vacation, is finding a suitable place that is quiet, and hasn't got many reflective audio surfaces to create nasty reverberations or echoes.
I tend to end up with a desk that's against a wall, and then put as many pillows as I can find upright against the wall, and then I would

put a duvet over my head while I record. I've recorded many important voice overs this way, and although it gets a bit stuffy under there, this can give remarkably good results. But – be aware that you won't have good monitoring equipment with you in the hotel room, so do a test with this kind of setup at home first, and then playback on your big speakers.

You may find that the recordings are hopelessly muffled and bassy. In the hotel room, it may sound perfectly OK playing back on the tiny little loudspeaker or on headphones there, but will sound awful when you send it to the production company in their studio. So at home, when you're in your own studio, work out what can fix this bass and muffled issue, and usually it's nothing more needed than a pre-set on your graphic or parametric equaliser. So take that pre-set with you, and apply it before you send the file off.

I would also suggest that you work out a pre-set for a decent software noise gate as well. Many hotel rooms have got some pesky background fan that you can't switch off, or distant rumble of traffic outside.

A decent noise gate can clean up a recording considerably in an environment like this. However, as I've mentioned before, don't use the noise gate that is in Adobe Audition, as once your audio levels go below a threshold, it cuts off completely, and then cuts IN completely when it hears your next word. With the Audition noise gate, it will cut off the starts of subtle word sounds like the "s" sound, so I recommend you use the free plug in from REASON, called the REAGATE. Download it to your computer, install it and then in Adobe Audition, scan for it in your plug-in manager. Then you apply it via the VST. The REAGATE is brilliant as it's a "soft" noise gate and doesn't suddenly switch on and off. It can "pre-sense" your next word and you can even mix "wet" and "dry" outputs. So once you have got the settings right at home, where you can playback your experiments on big loudspeakers, save that as a pre-set as well, and apply the software noise gate to clean up your hotel room recordings.

40
MARKETING YOUR VOICE – GET MORE WORK

Even you have a fantastically trained voice, you're a wonderful presenter, you have a broadcast quality studio and you're the fastest and most accurate audio editor in the known universe, nobody will know about you and you won't be successful financially unless you tackle the marketing issue.

First of all, let me remind you of the two "types" of voiceover. If you have an agent with an "exclusive" deal, they should do most of the marketing for you. If you have an exclusive agent, if you're approached by a client directly to record a voiceover, under the terms of your arrangement, you would normally have to refer them to your agent. If you are approached by another agent for a job, you would also refer them to the original agent you have the exclusive deal with.

You would also not be allowed to post your services on voiceover directory sites like Voices.com, Bodalgo, Voice 123 and so on. If you have your own website, the only contact numbers and emails will those of your agent – only! This saves you any hassle dealing with bookings and invoicing, and your agent will know other potential and confirmed bookings for you, so nothing gets double booked. The other major advantage is that you may find it difficult to put a decent fee on your services, so your agent will be able to negotiate for you often an amount far more than you would maybe have dared to suggest, so even with the agent's commission, you still earn more on that job.

The other type is the fully independent voiceover like myself. You would not be under any exclusive agreement with anybody, but you could certainly have many "non-exclusive" agents looking out for work for you.

To be honest, you will find as an independent, most of your income will come, not from being on voice websites with loads of other voices as competition, but from the solid relationships you will make with studios and producers who will hire you direct, and will not even think of auditioning anyone else for your type of voice.

So earlier, I got you set up with your "shop window" of your professional and functional voiceover website, you've got some decent showreels on there, so what next? It's time to contact people who don't know about you!

Cold contacting is called "cold" because you have had no previous contact with the person you are about to email or telephone. It can sometimes take a lot of effort to warm up your client so they then become a hot lead, and then turn into a client who will give you voiceover work. Once you have had at least one job with the client, it makes it so much easier in contact with that person, to get repeat business.

The reason we are voice artists is because it's enjoyable, it's very satisfying when we get the voice tone and subtle nuances plus the split-second timings just right as the client was looking for and it's nice when those payments come in to reward us! However, success does not happen automatically or magically, and to be honest, marketing is rarely fun or satisfying. We all know that without letting people know about our existence and our skills, we're just not going to have a career at all. So, do you think of marketing as a necessary evil? Maybe that's not quite the right phrase to use.

Let's start with cool, logical thought about this. We all know that marketing is essential, but we can always make excuses as to why we don't want to do marketing "quite yet". After all, maybe our showreels could be improved, or there's that fairly important demo we need to record, or we'll just have another coffee, or we'll go for a quick walk to get some air, you know what I'm on about here!

Let me put to bed what seems like an easy fix to voiceover marketing. There are for sale, right now, many email lists you can buy from the net that purport to be of production companies and advertising agencies that need voiceovers. Now, who in their right mind would buy one of these email lists? I'd like to bet that many of the email addresses are dead now or never did exist, and why would you be emailing the exact same list as scores or hundreds of OTHER voice talents?

So don't even think of buying one of these lists and then contacting an email marketing company with your needs to send out a huge mass mailing to probably vaguely relevant media people. This will rarely work at all. At best it will be waste of time and money, at worst, there may be some genuine good future contacts who are going to be really fed up with what will seem to be another impersonal message from "that darn email list".

Look, I have to be frank here. There are no short cuts. To get real results, you have to do it the hard way, and you can't put it off until "another time" as that time funnily enough never arrives! I'm just as guilty at procrastinating as the other voice artist, as it's always more attractive to do things that are fun than the, to be honest, often awkward and sometimes scary aspects of cold contacting potential new clients.

So, let's assume we don't have procrastination or laziness issues, but surely isn't it a better use of our time to outsource marketing to people we can pay, who don't find it a pain to do, or even enjoy it, and we can do voiceover recordings all day? You may find an experienced marketing expert, but if they did know the voice business well, they'd be a voice agent themselves. Would you really trust somebody else to sell your voiceover services if they didn't know exactly what they were selling? No. You need to get to start and nurture relationships with future clients, and you can only do that yourself. If it's that much of a problem for you, then go the first route and find an exclusive agent and you may be lucky. Or do it all yourself and CREATE your own luck!

So we're talking about one to one relationships here. With a big production company or ad agency, there may be one person who deals with booking voiceovers for projects, or there may be a number of creative directors who all have the freedom to choose voices for their personal projects. So you need to play detective with every company you contact and record what you find out when you call or email each one.

This is where a CRM system comes into play, unless you want to deal with reams of paper with notes or Excel files which really aren't suitable for this sort of work. CRM stands for Customer Relationship Management, and there are a few systems specifically aimed at voiceovers! Some CRM systems will offer a crazy amount of features that you may not really need, such as an autoresponder service, survey capabilities, configurable metric reporting, integration with social media, contact list integration and so on.

I say "may" not really use, as you may be the kind of outward going kind of person who shares all sorts of interesting things on social media already, so regular mail outs to all your contacts will be natural to you. Some programs like Comf5 even offer an easy way to send video emails to people, if you really want to do this.

For me, personally, I'm not that sort of person, and for me, I feel uncomfortable sending out mass emails to everyone in my database, listing interesting or prestigious jobs I've recorded recently, with maybe some news of availability. It just seems impersonal to me, and also for some clients who, say, work just in radio, they'd not be interested at all about the TV ads I've voiced, and vice versa. So, even though it takes much longer, I do every one of my marketing messages by email individually, still using basic templates, but customising every one to make them hit the targets more effectively.

So it's all horses for courses, here are some of the CRM systems and you just need to check out these to find any that could offer the features you need for your own personality and needs.
Comf5
Constant Contact
Insightly
Mail Chimp
Highrise
Apptivo
Zoho CRM
Big contacts
RatePoint
SalesForce CRM
Voiceoverview.com

Now out of all of these, the one I think is most useful for voiceovers is called voiceoverview.com, and if you check out the webpage you see that it offers a one-page website free of charge, and the facilities so you can track how many demos you've done, how many have been translated into actual work and how much you've been paid. The whole CRM system is aimed at the voiceover, and it is quite easy to use. And you may absolutely love this. For me personally, my client data base is on my XERO cloud-based accounting system, but that's me, and you may find that a good CRM system will keep you organised – but organised you do have to be, even if you use clipboards and paper or Excel.

The question I'm asked a lot is whether you should cold call by phone or by email. It's not a cop out to say... it depends! Let's say you found a website of an advertising agency that have some really cool videos and TV spots that they've produced. Usually these kinds of websites have an "about us" page. Here you may find photographs of creative directors and links to various TV spots they have made.

They could well be some productions that you have known from the television or cinema, and you may well have been impressed. You may find a direct email to that creative director, in which case you have a golden opportunity to email them direct, very briefly saying you came across their website and wanted to congratulate them on the project that you liked. You would then say by the way, "I am a professional voice talent, check out my website if you have time". This technique has worked many times for me, and I've had positive replies with my showreels going into their roster. You see, people like to be congratulated for work they have done, and they are proud of. You may have to tell a few little white lies, but for companies and organisations who have got media on their websites, the technique of asking a question or two praise the work, gives you a reason to contact them.

Okay, so let's say you found a similar website, you found the creative director, but there is no direct email address to that person. This is where you call up the switchboard, and you simply ask to speak to that creative director. You will often be asked who you are and what is the reason for your call. Here is your chance to use your gift of the gab, and not quite lie, but you would say you just wanted to ask a quick question about a project he or she has created.

Don't feel scared about calling switchboards, normally the person who is on a switchboard is to be honest, often bored, and as long as you are friendly and professional and clear, it's amazing how easy it is to get through what is in effect a gatekeeper.

With anyone you contact, either by email or by phone, you have to show an interest in what they are doing, it can't be all one-way. You are not just saying *"Hello I am here, I am talented, use me!"* You are also saying, let's work together on future productions, I can add value to your future productions, and what's more, I would be proud and inspired to work with you, especially having seen the work on your website. That is the sort of angle you need to take in your communication, but you need to say it YOUR way. Another way to think about it, is to take the angle of helping people. Think what can you do for that person? So, thinking like that, you might like to say to a potential new client:

"Do you have any projects coming up soon where I could offer a free custom demo you could play to your client? I'd be happy to help you out."

I know in production companies and advertising agencies, quite often they put together very rough demos of TV ads or radio commercials and use in-house people to do the voice-overs, simply because they're free. But if you are offering to do this for free anyway, and you're a professional voice-over, with a professional microphone and studio, wouldn't they bite your hand off? With a great voice on it, recorded properly, not on an iPhone in an office, wouldn't the client be more likely to accept the demo?

I know it is not easy. It does take time, effort, and sometimes a lot of detective work, to find the right people who will like you and put you on their books. And then it takes a bit more determination to stay in touch, so they will remember you when a job that is suitable for your voice comes up!

When you start off your voice-over career, you will probably need to spend 75% of your time doing nothing else but marketing. This would include doing demos, and searching for actual specific jobs day by day. As time goes on, and as you get your regular clients on board, you can drop that amount down so it becomes about 50% of your total time doing marketing. It never stops of course, and you need to keep that pot boiling. I do about 10% of my time mining new clients for the future.

I think it's important not to have a negative mindset, you need to think that generally people are nice, open, and want to hear what you have to say. Don't feel that you are pestering people by phoning them or emailing them. You have a service, a good service, and you will be adding value to their productions by doing a good job.

A word about social media. LinkedIn is great for finding creative directors, film producers and production managers of film and TV commercial production companies. Invite them to join your network. When they reply, send them a customised boilerplate message saying thanks for joining your network and please check out your voiceover website. Apart from LinkedIn, Twitter can be useful especially for following ad agencies and production companies for commercials and video games where often job opportunities are posted.

When you do get a really prestigious job, you do have the desire to want people to know about it to add credibility to your own voice-over brand. But I think using social media to brag about every big job is the wrong way to go about it. It's far better to be subtle about it. For example, when I've got three or four new TV commercials made, I put them on my voice-over website via Vimeo embedding. Then there is a reason for me to contact people by email, to mention that I have updated my website with various new showreels and a few new TV spots. Keep the tone casual, the length of the message short, and they might be intrigued to visit your website again, but it doesn't really matter. It's a reason to contact them. You must continually mention to people who haven't used you yet that you are willing to do a free custom demo for anything suitable they have on at the moment.

So where do you start with marketing? It's all about slow relationship building. As I say, forget bought "lists". You ideally need to tread with no other voiceover has tread before! In the forthcoming chapters I'll give you a great tip how to target production companies looking for voiceovers. Remember, the world is your marketplace. So many voiceovers make the mistake of only targeting their city, or even their country. We are very lucky, in that we speak the English language. Virtually every country in the world has a need for media to be translated and recorded into English. So find a country, picking at random if you like, Iceland, Romania, wherever! Now use your favourite search engine, and you'll be surprised how many media and production companies, audio studios, and individual producers are out there, some maybe just starting out, and are desperately looking for professional voiceovers who can speak native English for their productions in a variety of styles and accents.

The other thing to say about this, is that as marketing goes on, you'll find yourself getting success types of voiceovers or niches, or even in countries. This is because your name gets spread around, or clients move from one company to another in the same niche, and suddenly you find yourself earning a lot of money from one particular type of voice style, or production. For example, I found myself getting a lot of work from German and Austrian production companies wanting me to do English versions of industrial or image films. So I put more marketing efforts into both the genre and those countries, and now I have a healthy income just from doing that. For you, it may be that you are a natural at doing e-learning, or fiction audiobooks, where you can do lots of different character voices, we are all different!

So cold contacting clients is something that has to be done, nothing will happen quickly, and it is something that you will have to invest time in over a year or two before you fully get up to speed. Of course you may get some really good lucky breaks in that time, but there are many famous, successful people who have reiterated the mantra that the harder you work, the luckier you get!

OK, so let's assume that you have done your "cold contact" work, and you've now got two lists. You would have a list of people who either didn't reply to your cold contact after a few weeks, or DID reply, but said that they had enough similar voices on their roster and wouldn't be taking anything any further. This list of contacts you would keep for the future, when different people may answer the phone or email. "NO" doesn't always mean "NO" for eternity! So, leave that list for a year's time or so.

So, for your second list, you would have a decent database of clients from round the world in production companies, advertising agencies, audio studios, and independent producers and so on, and these people have responded positively to you in one of two ways.

Firstly, they may have actually had a suitable script for your voice when you cold contacted them, and you actually did the job and got paid, and they loved you! So you just need to remind them after a suitable gap, say a couple of months or so if you haven't heard back, that you are still around and available for more. This is where a CRM system comes into play as it can remind you to do things – or just write it into a physical diary if you wish.

Or, secondly, when you cold contacted them, they may have said: *"Thanks, you have a good voice and we haven't a voice like yours on our roster. We'll be in touch, but we don't have anything right now."* So how do you keep in touch with people? Do you fear that if you call up people or email them they are going to get fed up with you and put you on their "pester" list? I once felt this, a lot actually! But then I thought, when has someone I called been ever angry with my call, or sounded like they were too busy to talk to me? I thought…, er…never! One client actually told me once that he actively looks forward to my calls and updates as they cheer him up so much!

What us voice talents must remember is that we offer a professional service that is valuable to clients. If you're working for an ad agency or production company, their "end client" who chose your voice, loves you very much, and so your direct client, that is, the production company who paid you, are going to as well!

Think of your talents that you offer everyone. Your voice will help transform the video they are working on, help beef up the commercial, get phones ringing, people clicking websites, delivering the end client's messages in an effective way and adding value to the whole project. That's what we all do and we should all feel very proud of this and the service we offer.

41
YOUR POTENTIAL FUTURE CLIENTS

This chapter is all about thinking of all the possible future clients you could be targeting as a voice talent. At the end of the book is my list of 50 applications, but let's start thinking from scratch. Some applications may offer pretty rare opportunities such as being the instructor voice in a defibrillator, a character voice in an electronic birthday card or announcing tram stops in a city or whatever, so let's think about general situations where you are more likely to get regular work.

First of all, the job that the average member of public thinks about when you tell them you're a voiceover, yes, commercials.

Radio and TV commercials are often written by advertising agencies because they have existing contracts with brands and organisations for all their advertising and often marketing needs, so when a radio or TV ad needs to be actually made, they'll need to outsource the production as ad agencies very rarely have their own recording facilities in house. So who actually chooses the voiceover for each job? Sometimes for smaller clients, it's the boss or represented colleagues at the brand that is being advertised, and they would want to actively choose a voiceover from auditions – usually, they start with wanting an A-List movie star or celebrity but after a look at the budget, there's then a discussion about the general style they're looking for! The sex, age and voice style would be discussed with the end client company and the advertising agency would normally be trusted to follow the guidelines to actually find the right voice talent.

Creative directors at advertising agencies will have their own voice favourites and they may choose from this list, but the audio or video production company they're using will also have their own roster of voiceovers, so it may be that the creative director will ask to hear demos from the production company as well.

So we as voiceovers have two possible targets here, but a word of warning in that the BIG ad agencies don't usually accept direct contact from independent voiceovers. With very high budget TV commercials, risk has to be mitigated. You'll find that the larger agencies with the more prestigious client lists will have a policy to work only with established voice agencies they will have had a good relationship with. Why? Imagine you're a creative director with a lot of pressure to get a brilliant multi million pound commercial produced in all the different areas of concept, writing, storyboarding, actor casting, locations, filming, CGI, editing and so on.

For the voiceover element of this huge project, the creative director will want to trust their favourite voice agency or agencies to get custom demos from all their voices of a certain type they're looking for. To deal with a load of independent voiceovers all in different locations can be a lot of hassle.

However, for small to medium sized projects, creative directors may well cast the net further especially when an unusual voice sound is needed. They may go to their roster of voices from independent voice artists who have contacted them directly and ask for custom demos, or use a voice website like Voices.com, Voice123.com, Mandy.com or Voice Realm where it gives the agency an easy way to check all the demos sent in by voice subscribers on one website page. I'm on all these leading sites and get some nice jobs sometimes that lead on to future direct work afterwards.

TV commercials are rarely produced by individual TV stations these days, who tend to just make promos for their own programmes, although these will need voice talents. Radio stations will tend to make some adverts in-house, but usually the larger radio stations will outsource advert production to dedicated commercial production houses, and the smaller stations may have such small budgets for commercial production they have to use radio presenters and other staff already on their books to save money. If you're an older or senior voice, you may have a better chance of working with smaller radio stations direct, as most staff presenters or DJ's may tend to be younger, so for the odd Santa or wizard voice, you could get a gig, but usually the pay for local and regional radio ads is not that great.

eLEARNING AND TRAINING – I love eLearning and training scripts, because I tend to learn a lot from doing the jobs, but I have to admit I get some very technical subjects or scripts so incredibly detailed, I often don't have a real clue about the meaning of what I'm saying. The key, of course, is to put the right emphasis on words and use the power of the pause, and it's remarkable how you can sound like you're a real expert on any script! So how do you get this work? A lot of general media production houses deal with this kind of work and there are some dedicated companies who only deal with training and eLearning work. You simply need to make contacts and get onto their roster of narrators. It helps if you DO have a working knowledge of the subject matter, so say this when you apply.

When contacting them, you'll need to send a showreel that features just training script material and emphasise that you have a quality studio to record at the very best quality. When quoting to eLearning companies by the way, you must make it very clear if your work includes file cutting, as many training companies need individual files for every line or sentence to fit their eLearning system. If you don't charge for this, you'll find yourself very much out of pocket as it sometimes takes ages to cut and to rename the files, even if you use the automated system in NCH Wavepad or other file cutting solutions.

WEB PROMOS and CORPORATE VIDEOS

Unless you're dealing with massive organisations with their own video and audio production studios, corporate films and web promos can be made by a whole variety of different people, any of which may make the decision on the voice-over. There are all sorts of different types of production companies, some may be "full service" ones, that deal with anything audio and video, or they could be some that specialise just in industrial films, and have got equipment to film in factories, with drones, and safety gear for the very heavy and dangerous work. Of course, you as a voiceover, don't really mind what the subject matter is about, but there are huge opportunities in this area, and you may find the vast majority of your work coming from this sort of area.

It's a big area because non-English films will almost always have to have an English version, so you're not dealing with just the English-speaking countries but virtually every other country under the sun will need an English language version.

So this is great news for translators, and it's great news for us English voice-overs.

PHONE PROMPTS
So many companies and organisations have sophisticated phone call routing systems these days, and maybe you've called up one of these and heard an awful amateur sounding voice, or a nasty computer voice recorded at a low level, distorted or swamped by loud annoying music, welcoming you to the company switchboard. If you feel you could do a better job, then offer your services! They'll listen to you more if you point out the damage to the company's brand values an unprofessional voice prompt can do as the first thing a customer hears.

They'll listen even more if you say you're a customer of their company, or if you are a local person to their business. Be tactful when pointing out their unprofessional existing phone prompts, after all, it could be the CEO's wife on them!

Offer to record some free demo phone prompts in your professional studio and mix with low level suitable copyright-free music. Make it sound as if they would be doing you a favour as you're trying out some new studio equipment, or whatever. If they love your demos, then record them all, asking what file type and data rate etc., their phone system uses. Be aware that clients generally don't like to pay a lot for phone prompts as they are "so short". Of course, you and I know they are a right pain to record properly, as most clients want friendly and casual style but keeping utmost clarity.

That clarity is so compromised by the nasty compression and distortion added by any phone system, and it's hard to get the right balance of colloquial style and enunciation. The upside is that if you become the "voice of an organisation" for the phone system, if you keep in touch, you could well be asked to voice the next corporate "image" video or even the next radio or TV commercials, so it's well worth getting into an organisation by using the phone prompt route.

When you make initial contact, you often don't actually have to complain about the poor existing voice prompts, the managers may well already know but just never "got round" to doing anything about it. A form of words you could use on the phone or in your initial email is *"I wonder if you've thought of using a professional voiceover for your phone system prompts for your company? The first thing a potential or existing customer hears when they call is so important to the integrity of any brand, and I'm an established voice talent with a broadcast quality studio used to recording quality phone messages."* Then after the response, you'd say something like *"Look, I've got a new studio mixer I'm testing out, can I record some free demos for you based on the words from your existing voice prompts? I won't charge you a penny, and I need to record and edit something anyway."* After that, if it's true, hit them with the sucker punch of you being an existing customer of their company or maybe you live down the road from them and you pass their company every day, etc. and you're in!

GAME CHARACTERS
If you're a voiceover without an acting background, you may feel the option of offering video game character lines will not be in your field of skills, but you may be surprised. Revisit the earlier section on Character Voices. You never know what you have within you!

MUSEUM AND ART GALLERY NARRATIONS
With digital playback machines and infra-red technology becoming so inexpensive now, many tourist destinations, museums and art galleries offer to hire out headphones to visitors or give them a QR code to download an app so they can listen on their own phone. If you know a larger destination that doesn't do this now, but feel that a permanent exhibit or gallery would really benefit from the feature, just be proactive and get in touch.

Even if you can't offer the whole turnkey installation, the venue will probably know good Audio Visual companies and it could all come to fruition. It really will help if you have a personal interest in art, sculpture, architecture, or whatever the venue features. It will help you to spot mistakes in the scripts, you could maybe suggest small additions and also you'll know how to pronounce the names of artists or contributors correctly. I've recorded many of these gallery narrations over the years, many across Europe as the "English" option, and the key is to make what is often a "dry as dust" script come alive with your passion and enthusiasm.

One of my regular customers actually came from being on holiday in Austria and picking up a leaflet on a bus for an "audio tours" app, where programs were well written but not voiced by a native English person. I contacted them and recorded a short demo and

I'm now their regular voiceover. So you're always looking out for opportunities!

THEME PARK ANNOUNCEMENTS
As a bolt-on to museum and art gallery narration, don't forget theme parks who all need phone prompts, loudspeaker announcements, character voices for the individual rides and events and of course the radio and TV ads. For each park you'll probably find one agency or production house that has responsibility for all this kind of media. My voice is currently the English voice on the loudspeakers and phone prompts of a couple of Middle Eastern theme parks and as safety announcements on many UK rides. This work is decently paid and is often fun to do; if you ever go on a coach tour up the volcanic Mount Teide, in Tenerife in the Canary Islands, you may well hear my voice explaining the history of the volcano in a voice as the mythical monster living inside it!

DOCUMENTARIES & FACTUAL TV PROGRAMMES
You need to be a particular type of voice to get into narration work for documentaries; most traditional documentary producers like to let their pictures and the structure drive the story, and if you have showreels with a lot of "announcer" work on, it could be thought that your voice could be a bit distracting for documentary work. So a showreel dedicated to just documentary work is essential to show that you respect the genre. Often an individual producer or director is responsible for all the creative input in their projects, so you could get lucky by targeting these people in a social media site such as LinkedIn.

Of course, you could contact organisations such as Discovery or the BBC, but you'll find many documentaries are not actually made in-house, but are just commissioned there. Many productions themselves are made by independent production companies. A good tip is to keep a pad of paper by the TV and write down the names of production companies that pop up in the credits, then

Googling and contacting them. I've got some excellent leads and actual jobs just by doing this.

VOICE OF GOD ANNOUNCEMENTS – AWARD CEREMONIES etc.
For this kind of work, targeting event organiser companies can be very fruitful. These organisations offer others a turnkey service to plan, book and actually run various events, ranging from conferences to prestigious award ceremonies. Most of these events will need a professional voiceover to welcome on stage key speakers or announce that delegates need to take their seats. These announcements will normally be recorded. However, for more complicated events, such as big award ceremonies, you will have to physically be at the event, sitting in the shadows with the technical crew, wearing headphones so you're directed by the showcaller, the event name for director. I've done quite a few of these things and you really have to keep your wits about you.

The reason you need to be there in person is that the scripts can often change. Some award winners may not have turned up, or not go to the stage when their name is called, or the running order can be changed at the last moment. On top of this stress, you may have unusual names to be called out so before the event, you'll be hunting the people's colleagues to discover how to pronounce their names correctly. On the upside, doing live work is so satisfying when you get it right, especially when you need to "pad" with announcements when something goes wrong. It gets paid well, you should get travel and accommodation paid for, and if you have any kind of live experience such as radio, you'll be able to do this easily.

DJ LINERS – RADIO ID WORK
We are long from the era when radio "jingles" were sung with compressed block harmonies, and most radio stations, both broadcast and internet stations, these days have a voiceover mixed with various sweeps and music stings.

To get this work, you could contact the same production houses that make radio commercials, but most of these station ID liners are made by one or two enthusiasts in each station who love doing all the mixing and often crazy audio manipulation modern contemporary music stations use. It's a case of calling up and hunting out names, and sometimes ID work comes up on "Pay To Play" voice sites. Unless you're going to be on a network station, the pay isn't usually that good, but to be the "voice" of a radio station or two is a nice thing to have on your resume.

42

DIGGING DEEP ON THE NET & SEARCH WORDS

Now if you've ever set up any kind of company in the Internet era, you've probably set up your website with a really good domain name, and got some fancy website designer to come along and create a stunning website for you. And yet when you first try and search for your website by putting in various keywords, you just can't find it there on the first couple of pages of Google. Even if you put in the actual name of your company word for word, your website still doesn't show. So you employ someone who is skilled in the black art of search engine optimisation, or SEO, you may be able to get your companies name somewhere on the first two or three pages, and with an awful lot of effort, you'll get featured in the list that first page.

So let's imagine, you are a newly formed media company, a production company, a translation company or so on, somewhere in the world, that produces corporate videos not just in the native language where you are, but also, as there is a great need for it, with an English version as well. In that company, you would need to find and set up a good roster of English speaking voice overs, with North American, British, Australian, Indian, South African and so on accents. You would need male, female, young, older, and maybe some character voices as well, who would speak over or dub various interviews in the non-English language.

So what would you do to find these voiceover artists? You may go on a voiceover website, like voices.com, or a freelancing site like Upwork. But it's a right pain, it will take you a while to audition people and to determine whether they would be good enough for your needs. Also, have they a good studio, and would they be reliable, and professional enough for you? Would they welcome a direct approach from an independent professional voice-over like yourself? Someone who has been trained in all aspects of professional work? Of course they would!

You see, this is a big mistake many voice artists fall into when they are researching companies to contact. Most people use the Google search engine, and put in similar keywords, and everyone lazily just takes the companies on the first page. There is also the mindset, that organisations on the first page of Google, are the most important, and usually they are, when we are doing searches for things for our personal life.

So, following our mantra of stepping when no one else has stepped, I suggest if you are using Google, to at least ignore the first couple of pages and start mining production companies that would employ voiceovers, further down the pecking order. You're not just looking for newly formed companies, but also companies that are so busy, or so successful, they haven't quite got round to getting a decent SEO person in yet, as they are maybe not really ready to expand the company, indeed at the moment, they don't need the business, so why bother SEO-ing? However they might well need your services!

But let's take this one step further. While most of the world uses Google, is there an alternative? There's a marvellous search engine called MillionShort.com. Let's put in a search term, say "production translation company Dubai". Now without choosing any finds to be removed, see the choice here in the search window, these are the companies everybody else will probably find on their first page using a major search engine. But Million Short saves you a lot of hassle clicking through the pages.

Let's click "remove the first 100" and do it again. Now we have a new list. Of course you still need to drill down into each of these websites to discover what it is they have to offer, but you can do that later. Now all you are doing is cutting and pasting interesting

URLs into, say, a word document, you can work on later. By the way, when you are working with non-English companies, and trying to find organisations who would employ you as a native English speaker, it can be very fruitful to put that word "translation" into any search term, as many production companies who specialise in English work are also a translation agency, or offer those services.

So back to Million Short and as well as a "hundred off", let's take " a thousand off". In other words, it will give you everything, but the first thousand finds will be not shown. So in summary, you are looking for uncharted territory. You need to find companies and individual producers who will want voice talent, and haven't full voiceover rosters; so don't do the obvious. Everybody else will find the obvious, and pester the heck out of them. I have honestly had enormous success with this system. New clients I have found become very long-standing ones, and give me regular work. If you want to find contacts who are more likely to welcome you with open arms right away, look for the not obvious, and the Million Short search engine is a great tool to help you!

SEARCH ENGINE ESSENTIALS
The way to use keywords you're going to put into your search engine is to use them as they are, and then with a place name at the front and / or afterwards. You'll be surprised what extra finds pop up after this. Remember you are looking for any production house, individual producer / director or media provider that will need voiceovers in English. Don't just think of English-speaking countries. Virtually every corporate film will need to have an English version at some point!
Be very methodical. For example, start your day saying *"Today I will find all production houses in Austria"*. So you'd search using, maybe:

Vienna media production company
Media production company Vienna

Then the same for other centres in Austria - Salzburg, Linz, Eisenstadt, Graz, etc.

You'll be cutting and pasting the URLs you find that look hopeful into a Word document that you'll go to later for visiting each site to dig deeper.

Now, let me tell you a great secret - how to find companies that a **Google.com** site WON'T find!

Force your browser to go to the native Google search engine for your target country. So for Austria, it would be www.google.at

Then in Google Translate you'd translate your key terms into the native language, German. "**Vienna media production company**" = "**Medienproduktionsfirma Wien**"
Enter this and the magic will unfold! You will find more companies you didn't see before. Of course you would still contact non-English companies writing in English unless you really are fluent, and they should reply to you in English.

ADVERTISING SEARCH WORDS:
(Please note when searching for TV and radio production companies, be aware there are "media" companies that sell airtime to clients only and do not actually produce the adverts)

TV commercial production
TV spot production
TV advert production
Media advertising companies

eLEARNING SEARCH WORDS:
Training and development companies
Training and development organisations
eLearning production
media production for training

training videos
training video production
multimedia training production
multimedia training providers
eLearn solutions

CORPORATE VIDEO SEARCH WORDS:

Corporate video production
Image film production
Media for business
Business film production
Video for business
Video for corporations
Media production companies

PHONE PROMPTS / IVR (Interactive Voice Response) SEARCH WORDS:

IVR production company
Telephone prompt production
Phone message recordings
Telephone system messages
Message recordings for phones
Phone and IVR production

GAME VOICE WORK SEARCH WORDS

Casting agencies for video games
Animation voiceover agency
Game voice casting

MUSEUM WORK SEARCH WORDS:

AV design and installation
Museum interactive exhibit design
Audio Visual for Museums and Art galleries
Gallery and Museum AV production
Art gallery narration services

AWARD CEREMONY – "VOICE OF GOD" WORK:
Event companies
Virtual event companies
Event planning
Event organisation
Conference and event organisation
Virtual conference and event organisation

The great thing with the list of keywords that you use can be reused with the name of a city or town added somewhere in the key phrase that you are searching for. And this can often bring up interesting and new results. And don't forget you can then flip down the pages you find and mine deeper, or even use MillionShort.com and you will find all sorts of different production companies, agencies and potential individual producers or directors who may well need your voice.

43
THE THREAT OF THE A.I. VOICE

This section is about AI or Artificial Intelligence as it relates to creating computer-generated voiceovers, and basically my own thoughts about it. It's not that long a section, and it's a subject really not for us to worry about too much in many respects. Technology has always moved on, and many jobs have naturally changed in the process. Artificial voices have been around for many years. In the 1970's and 1980's, Sonovox or Vocoder voices were all the rage to enhance music recordings.

Even I had a minor pop hit across Europe writing and performing a record called "It Happened Then". You're welcome to listen to it, I think it's still on YouTube under my group name "Electronic Ensemble". The record was all me playing synthesizers multitracked, and the lead vocal music "tune" was played on a synth and then was played back through two tiny loudspeakers, in fact they were tweeters bought from Radio Shack. These tweeters playing the "tune" were pressed hard against my throat while I mouthed the words of the song as these little buzzing speakers created the robot voice in my voice box. A microphone placed very close to the mouth, picked up the results and that was recorded for the lead vocal track. The robot voice wasn't that clear, but it was an unusual sound, and as I say, it was released across Europe and had a lot of radio play, although I haven't actually bought a yacht on the proceeds yet!

Sonovox, using this technique has been used for radio liners and jingles as well, and also Vocoder used by people like Kraftwerk where the human voice has been synthesized from various tone and hiss generators.

But of course both these two systems, still need a human being to actually drive the sound. In other words, someone has to be playing a keyboard or mouthing the words while creating these voices. The Holy Grail for innovators in this world was always creating "text to speech" at a click of a button, an instant voiceover!

Of course, these days we do have that, from various providers, and the results are pretty average, but for many people it's acceptable for the type of project they have. Maybe they have low budget training projects, or basic low priority telephone prompts, and that's fine if that's all they want. But it does take a lot of time and technology to create each new "voice". So for companies who don't really want that organization represented by a flat, slightly distorted voice that sounds like it's from a satellite navigation device, and the exact same voice that's ALSO used by their competitors, they will always use a real human voice to represent their brand even if we cost more.

So I don't think that Artificial Intelligence, where it takes the text to speech system further, is that much of a threat at least for the next 10 or even 20 years. I really mean that, and it's not that I'm a Luddite at all. It's just that for so many scripts, the majority of them if you think about it, emotion is very important. It's the pride that has to come across in a corporate video, it's the selling technique of the commercial, and for all kinds of acting where there are so many different emotions at play, many of them subtle but important.

Yes, these emotions ARE possible to be programmed into an A I voice, and you can hear examples online now if you look for them, (on YouTube, for example, you can hear "FAITH – the First A.I. that can cry". This is impressive, but it's strange that the music is mixed quite high, probably to hide the artefacts on this artificial voice, and I wonder how long it took them to actually create this voice.) but when time is tight for a media project, isn't it easier for a client to explain something to a human, who "gets" you right away, rather than wait days or weeks for a programmer to get the computer to do the same?

So my advice to you if you are a little wary of computers taking over our jobs, is to try and get more and more types of scripts, where it's much harder for the computer to replicate the human voice, that is in voice acting, and any type of script where subtle human emotion is very important...and also in directed voice sessions, be cheerful and chatty and make the director's job easy and fun in between the takes. I've yet to hear a computer voice that's good on small talk or telling gags!

44

VOICEOVER DIRECTORIES & "PAY TO PLAY" SITES

Let's go back to basics first. When you're a professional voiceover, there are three ways you'll get scripts sent to you for you to record in return for cash.

1) **EXCLUSIVE AGENT** – usually actors or celebrities who voice part-time choose this option, simply put, they just wait for the phone to ring.

2) **INDEPENDENT VO** – you generate direct relationships with clients at production companies, you get non-exclusive agents to represent you and you get regular work from these people who trust you.

3) **VOICEOVER WEBSITES** – Voice directories of talents, some free and some you subscribe to, sometimes called "Pay to Play". There are loads of these sites out there, and here are 20 of the most active sites where you can sign up and wait for work to come to you.

Every site is different, here are the variations you'll find:

FREE TO JOIN

Just as it says, you don't pay any subscription, but the site will make their money from the end client, and / or taking a percentage from your voiceover fee.

SUBSCRIBE TO JOIN

Here you will need to pay, so you'll have to take a punt on whether you feel it's a good investment or not. These are usually sites where you have to audition for jobs, so make sure you have time to do this daily, or it's a waste of a fee.

DIRECT CONTACT

This is where the voiceover website puts you in touch with the client who likes your voice from your profile or your audition for specific jobs, and you send files and invoices direct to the client. Payment is unfortunately not guaranteed if you have a client who is not honest, the directory website is not involved or liable.

JOB DONE ON SITE

On these sites you do everything on the website and you'll often have to stay anonymous. You upload your audio files to the website, and you also get paid from the website. Payment guaranteed once the job is done well.

YOU BID FOR EACH JOB

You determine how much you will do the job for and you usually bid against other voice talents. Bidding low does not automatically get you the gig!

FIXED FEES BY WEBSITE

No matter how experienced you are or what you want your rates to be, the fee is fixed by the voice website and you get paid from that site too.

AUDITION FOR JOBS

Here, you'll create auditions that join the many others from the voiceover community, so your demo has to be good!

NO AUDITIONING REQUIRED

On sites listed here that feature this, you will have already been chosen from the showreels on your voiceover profile, so the job is highly likely to be yours.

fiverr®

https://www.fiverr.com/
https://www.fiverr.com/pro

NO AUDITIONING REQUIRED
JOB DONE ON SITE
FREE TO JOIN

On Fiverr you DON'T generally need to audition with voice artists. If a client comes on Fiverr and they find you and like the sound of your voice showreels and your general style, very rarely will they ask to you audition with anybody else, they normally are the type of fast turnaround small production studio who take a punt on you and the job is yours. Remember that you don't have to sell anything for just a paltry $5, where you actually only trouser $4. Your minimum fee can be $20 for 20 words if you like, so with all the EXTRAS for an average script like 200 extra words, a high quality WAV file, proof checking English translations, and the big money maker the "same day delivery" for, say $50 extra, which virtually EVERY client selects, an average job on Fiverr is about $200+.

What's more, there is now the FIVERR PRO service which is a bit of a "VIP club" and the suppliers go through a rigorous testing process and the clients are fully prepared to pay far more than the average service.

There is no annual subscription. Every separate type of job you create on Fiverr has to be called a separately named "gig".

https://studio.envato.com/

NO AUDITIONING REQUIRED
JOB DONE ON SITE
FREE TO JOIN

Envato Studio is set up for creative arts and I've been a featured voiceover on here for a few years. Like Fiverr, the quality of clients is pretty good, and I get voice jobs from all round the world who are prepared to pay fair fees for fairly easy jobs, and there is no subscription.

Also like Fiverr, in fact like every voice site apart from the frankly annoying system at Voice Bunny, you can freely communicate with the end clients and ask for pronunciation guide files or extra information regarding what they need.

Unlike Fiverr where you can draw out any "cleared" funds whenever you like, on Envato Studio you get paid every month as long as your income is over the threshold.

Voices.com

https://www.voices.com/

JOB DONE ON SITE
SUBSCRIBE TO JOIN
YOU BID FOR EACH JOB
AUDITION FOR JOBS

Voices.com, based in London, Canada. A really good quality site with some lovely jobs on there, a wide range of interesting projects of all types and good rates of pay.

Yes, you have to subscribe, but there are plenty of jobs targeted at both North American and British accents and support is first class. The Escrow system means your cash is safe until the client accepts your recordings.

https://voice123.com/

DIRECT CONTACT
SUBSCRIBE TO JOIN
YOU BID FOR EACH JOB
AUDITION FOR JOBS

Voices123.com is of the type of site that simply puts you in touch with the client, there is no Escrow; once the client choses you from your audition, you email or call them direct and sort out the job, and you invoice them afterwards direct.

Like Voices.com there are loads of interesting and lucrative jobs daily from round the world and you do have to pay an annual fee to be on the site.

https://www.thevoicerealm.com/voice-over-jobs-online.php

JOB DONE ON SITE

FIXED FEES BY WEBSITE

FREE TO JOIN

AUDITION FOR JOBS

Voice Realm also have good quality clients and a variety of types of jobs, and they have fixed rates so no bidding or temptations to undercut other voiceovers.

You're allowed to use your first name, but that's all…. and if there is a hint that you've tried to give contact details to the end client, you'll be thrown off the site. Take this seriously…don't do it.

There's a cool feature where you can switch on the "IN STUDIO" slider that stays on for 6 hours, so clients with urgent jobs know you're there in the booth waiting!

www.voplanet.com

JOB DONE ON SITE
SUBSCRIBE TO JOIN
YOU BID FOR EACH JOB
AUDITION FOR JOBS

VO Planet is a subscription site with high value jobs, and mostly for North-American voices.
There are occasional jobs for British & European voices.
The rates are fixed but you can in fact bid for MORE than the rate offered for each job, but you can't UNDER-bid!

THE VOICEOVER MARKETPLACE

https://voiver.com/

VOIVER is a Spanish site with a good selection of voiceovers including all accents of English, but mostly North American and British.

They have fixed fees and some interesting jobs, mostly corporate.

You do the whole job on the Voiver site and you send the invoice to Voiver at the end of each job.

JOB DONE ON SITE
FREE TO JOIN
FIXED FEES BY WEBSITE

WEBAUDIOSTORE is down the road from Spain in Portugal and has thousands of voiceovers on its directory site of all styles.

It also has fixed fees and you do all the work on the website communicating with the client via the WEBAUDIOSTORE site.

You're not allowed to give your direct contact details to clients.

https://www.bodalgo.com/en

DIRECT CONTACT
SUBSCRIBE TO JOIN
YOU BID FOR EACH JOB
AUDITION FOR JOBS

Over in Germany you'll find Bodalgo, and when you get a casting call from them, it's open season and you have to reply fast or else you'll see that literally hundreds of people have auditioned for the same job. Will the client listen to the early ones or the later ones, or all of the auditions?   You will often never know.

High value jobs are often on here, mostly from German companies and British and International accents are often needed.

http://outspokenvoices.com/

JOB DONE ON SITE
FREE TO JOIN
FIXED FEES BY WEBSITE

In the UK, there is OUTSPOKENVOICES.COM.

It's free to join, you need to pass a quality test for quality of equipment and voice standards and there's an escrow system when you get a job. In other words, you get paid from Outspoken once the end client is fully happy with your recording.

https://www.voquent.com/

JOB DONE ON SITE
FREE TO JOIN
FIXED FEES BY WEBSITE
AUDITION FOR JOBS

Also in London, this is VOQUENT - what they have realised is that a client is more likely to book a voiceover if they hear EXACTLY what they want so there are no general mixed showreels allowed – only short clips of a specific voice style, or clips for a very specific use. Sometimes you are asked to audition, but usually clients will like you and book you there and then.

https://www.mandy.com/jobs/auditions/uk/voiceovers

DIRECT CONTACT
SUBSCRIBE TO JOIN
YOU BID FOR EACH JOB
AUDITION FOR JOBS

Another London site is MANDY.com and the voiceover section there has many interesting and quite well paid UK jobs for mainly British accent voice talents.

Many London agencies source their voice talents from the Mandy site.

I strongly suggest you list yourself on Mandy VOICES and Mandy ACTORS as well, as quite often voice jobs get posted on the "Actors" one as clients either get confused or don't know the difference. The acting jobs usually are more fun anyway!

www.peopleperhour.com

JOB DONE ON SITE
FREE TO JOIN
YOU BID FOR EACH JOB
AUDITION FOR JOBS

People Per Hour is a London based general freelance site but there are plenty of voiceover jobs on there. Beware though, the site attracts some low value ones which you should ignore even if you're starting out. At least there is no subscription to join.
It's bit of a clunky interface but if you can find your way around you could get some good well-paid jobs here.

https://www.fivesquid.com/search/voiceovers

JOB DONE ON SITE
FREE TO JOIN
YOU BID FOR EACH JOB
NO AUDITIONING REQUIRED

Also a British site called "fiveSquids.com" is arguably a poor man's Fiverr site but you can sell your voiceovers on there as long as you play the same trick as you would on Fiverr, in other words make sure the £5 is for a TINY script with LONG delivery time so the extras like "delivery today" which most clients will want, make it worthwhile doing for you.

www.voicesuk.co.uk
www.voicesus.com

JOB DONE ON SITE
FREE TO JOIN
YOU BID FOR EACH JOB
AUDITION FOR JOBS

Voicesuk.co.uk has an escrow system so you don't have to chase the end clients for cash and it's aimed at British voices, and it also has a North American sister site at **voicesus.com** for American and Canadian accents.
Some nice and interesting jobs pop up from time to time and there is no subscription, you just need to show you're a professional.

V🎙ICEOVERS.com

www.voiceovers.com

In the United States, a site that has very high standards is
www.Voiceovers.com where there are no open casting calls, you
wait to be invited to audition and there are very low numbers of
voiceovers of each voice style and accent allowed and they have to
pass a stringent quality test.

JOB DONE ON SITE
FREE TO JOIN
FIXED FEES BY WEBSITE
AUDITION FOR JOBS

www.Voicecrew.com may tickle your fancy; it's mostly North American voices that are needed but other accents are sometimes required.

The rates are pretty low but if you get a batch of scripts it could be worth your while. At least you don't pay to join.

Many Voices, One Goal.

www.voicejockeys.com

JOB DONE ON SITE
FREE TO JOIN
FIXED FEES BY WEBSITE
AUDITION FOR JOBS

Voice Jockeys have jobs that will give you about $50 for a full buy-out rate and other pretty low value voice jobs; but to be fair, most of the scripts are short and easy to do. Mostly North American accents required here.

www.voicejungle.com

JOB DONE ON SITE
FREE TO JOIN
FIXED FEES BY WEBSITE
NO AUDITIONING REQUIRED

Voice Jungle are America-based but use all sorts of English accents! They are often interesting scripts offered and they love fast responses and they have now introduced a premium service for even faster recordings, which costs the client more, but gives you more too.

https://www.upwork.com/freelance-jobs/voice-over/

JOB DONE ON SITE
FREE TO JOIN
YOU BID FOR EACH JOB
AUDITION FOR JOBS

Upwork started life as Elance and O'Desk years ago and they joined forces. In theory it should be a quality site attracting quality clients but unfortunately it attracts clients who just want cut price deals, some offering insultingly low rates, like $50 for an hour of an audiobook or something.

There are SOME clients who are prepared to pay normal rates so it's worth being on there, but even though there is no formal subscription rate, you do have to buy "connects" in order to bid for jobs. You can just wait for a client to find your profile and showreels and make you an offer, but don't ignore this site; sometimes very high-profile voice jobs are advertised here. Be aware that the site interface and design is appalling; I've been on it for years and still often can't find where to click for things!

Other voiceover sites you may like to check out:
www.pickavoice.com
https://www.voicebunny.com
www.voiceoverdirect.com
www.voicehunter.com
http://www.directvoices.com/
www.voiise.com
https://www.premiumvoices.com/
https://www.voiceover.biz/
https://www.cheapvoiceover.biz/
http://www.cheapvoicetalentonline.com/ (Same company as
Voice Realm)
www.great-voices.com
www.voxendo.com
www.justvoicesagency.com
http://www.bh.bighousecasting.com/submissions/
www.voicetalentonline.com
www.voiceover.cafe
www.speaker-search.co.uk
http://www.shiningvoices.com/faq.php
www.vsi-london.tv
www.voicearchive.co.uk
www.matinee.co.uk
http://www.voicegroup.com/cont.html
www.voicesquad.com
www.voicecrafters.com
www.mediagroup.com.au
www.stimmgerecht.com
http://www.gmvoices.com/
https://voicegiant.com/
www.adelphitranslations.co.uk
http://www.voicetalentonline.com/
https://en-gb.thebigword.com/translation-
localisation/multimedia-services/
https://voiceresort.com/voice-over-speak

http://www.vopstudio.com/join-our-vo-team/
https://www.mediamusicnow.co.uk/help-support/supplier-enquiry/voiceovers.aspx
http://www.acx.com/ (AUDIO BOOKS ONLY)
https://www.gamedevmarket.net
(YOU CREATE STOCK VOICES FOR GAMES & SELL HERE)

https://www.productiontrax.com/contribute.php
(YOU CREATE STOCK VOICES FOR GAMES & SELL HERE)

https://epicstockmedia.com/contributor-interest/
(YOU CREATE STOCK VOICES FOR GAMES & SELL HERE)

The above subscription and free VO websites may give the impression that they offer an easy way of getting work, but neither the free or the subscription sites will give you a full-time income. Consider these sites to be the "icing on the cake", and we estimate that an average VO will get about 20% of their income from sites like these even if you are on most of them. At the end of the day, you can't beat direct relationships with direct clients who will use you again and again.

45
FIFTY JOBS A VOICEOVER COULD DO

So how many types of job could a voice artist do? I've put together this list from jobs I have done myself, but I'm sure you can add some voice uses I have not included that maybe you've done!

Animation character voices
Art Gallery audio guide
Audio description on TV /cinema for visually impaired
Audiobooks
Award ceremony VOG announcements
Children's apps
Cinema commercials
Conference speech introductions
Corporate image films
Documentary narration
Escape rooms voiceovers
Explainer videos
Factual Audiobooks
Fiction Audiobooks
Game characters
Game narration
Hypnosis recordings
In-store / mall announcements
IVR- Telephone recordings
Lift / elevator announcements
Museum audio guide
Narrator in a musical / play
News reading
Non-English drama lip-sync replacement
Non-English interview non-sync replacement
Podcast intros and outros
Poem narrator for YouTube

Point of sale videos in shops
Promo narrations
Radio commercials
Radio drama acting
Radio presenter links
Radio station Idents
Rail station / Port / Airport announcements
Reversing truck warnings
Relaxation recordings
Safety announcements at an activity centre such as a trampoline park
Sat Nav recording
Speaking clock
Stadium announcements
Store "Tannoy" announcements
Talking greeting cards
Talking newspapers for visually impaired
Theme park announcements
Timed sectional voiceover scripts
Tourist audio guides
Training course narration
TV commercials
TV continuity
Voice in a toy or medical device
YouTube channel narrator

46

TEN QUICK TOP TIPS FOR VOICEOVERS

Finally, here are ten tips mined from this book, in no particular order of importance, and are, in my opinion, unusual ones that you will rarely find elsewhere. These tips have made my life easier, and more efficient in many ways, recording and editing voiceover scripts for a profession.

TIP 1
First of all, have two audio software programmes on your computer. Why is this?
It's basically so you got one to record and one to playback. If you do a script which has quite a few unusual names in there, your client may well send you an extensive audio file with recordings of how to pronounce the names.

So how are you going to play them, if you are already recording in your software programme? So what I do, is to have the very latest updated version of Adobe Audition on my computer to record and edit on, and a really old copy of Adobe Audition, actually it's 1.5 actually, and I installed it off a CD ROM can you believe!   And in my computers default programmes, I make sure that when I click on an MP3, or a WAV file as sent from a client, it always opens in the old program. This is because, most of the time when you open any audio file, it's because it's sent from the client, either as a reference file, or for as a pronunciation guide. For a long tourist guide with many non-English names, it is a right pain to stop recording and to open up the pronunciation file again, and to see a waveform on your screen is simply easier to navigate than if you have opened up the guide file in VLC media player or whatever that you'd flip to. So, with two audio software programmes, that are completely separate, you keep recording, and flip between the two programs using ALT + TAB.

TIP 2

When you're shopping for clothes for work, don't just look for clothes that look smart, but sound smart! You don't want to have any clothes that make nasty rustling noises. If you do this, you'll be **aware** of those pesky rustling noises when you are recording your voiceover scripts, then you'll tense up, and not give your best performance. Soft cloth that doesn't rustle is the best choice for a voiceover artist. Better still, as nobody can see you, strip off and do it top naked!

TIP 3

If you've got a very softly spoken script to read and you're aware that your breathing is rather noisy, try using an "Easy Breathe" metal strip to widen your nasal passages. These sprung metal devices stick on your nose and are designed to help you breathe better in bed through the nose so you don't open your mouth and snore, but for us voiceovers, they are lifesavers in front of the microphone, especially if you have a very soft, intimate script where you're directed live and you can't stop and edit out breaths afterwards. Of course you can also wear them in bed, and this makes it less certain that you will sleep with your mouth open, and give you a sore throat for the morning. Try them!

TIP 4

As well as recording on the computer, via your USB interface, also record completely separately on a solid-state recorder, with an input level slightly less than that of the input to the computer. 99% of the time, you will just use what you have recorded on the computer, but that odd peak of volume that distorts on your computer, may be perfectly ok if you use the recording on the solid-state machine. In my voice booth, I've got it set up this way, and it's amazing how often you do need to use the backup recording. It's wired up so that the microphone output goes into a "Y" lead where one output goes into the computer via the USB interface, and the other wire goes directly into the solid-state recorder. This is my "worry-free" "Belts and Braces" system!   Nothing can possibly go wrong!

TIP 5
Don't send the invoice in with the recording! There may be some changes needed, maybe you recorded something wrong, the client may change their mind over the script, but more likely you're going to slightly annoy the client asking for money before even they have got paid from their own end client. So unless you have specifically been asked to send in the invoice, just wait patiently until you get the full all-clear from the feedback on your recording, and then send it in. You will be much more respected from your agency, and more likely to be thought of positively for future jobs. So don't be money grubbing, or appear desperate for cash, just have a decent system of remembering when you've done jobs, and invoicing them when they are complete. You can either use an Excel sheet, or a simple sheet of paper on a clipboard.

TIP 6
When recording an audition, where they have insisted that you read all the audition script, don't be suspicious and think they're just going to steal the whole recording, so you just do half of it. It could be that they want to show the end client the video with your entire voice over in, before they make a decision. It is highly unlikely a professional client will steal the demo recording from you, so read it all, and not only will this help you to get the job, but it will stop the situation where, if you had only supplied half the script, you'll have to match the exact voice style and resonance that you recorded in the first part that they loved, to the new part you will now have to record!

TIP 7
Always wire up your studio and have a system so you always keep the original unprocessed audio file. Even if most of your clients don't mind the hardware noise gate you use or compression, you

will come across studios who demand the original raw file from you. You won't be able to provide this if your microphone is plugged into the effects box first, will you? So if your recording location has low level hum or rumble that you are using a hardware Noise Gate to remove at source, do this in software after recording if you have to. Always keep the original unprocessed audio file. Maybe it's another use for a "Y" XLR lead!

Tip 8

Get physical in the voice booth! Your performance will be far better if you learn to express the words you are saying with your arm and hand movements. Underline in the air the words that are meant to be emphasised or punch the air for power "hit" words. Use actual ironic speech marks in the air when appropriate, and make all the facial expressions you like to convey the emotion of the script whether it is acting or narration. Your performance will be enhanced enormously by physically "acting out" what you're saying by your upper body!

TIP 9

Always make a great first impression. If you're recording and editing voiceover scripts in the order that they come in, and you're in the middle of an urgent job to do for an existing client, what do you do if suddenly an enquiry comes in from a potential new client? Yes of course, you would just take 2 minutes out to reply to that new client, and they will be impressed with your speed of response and you'll probably get the job. There's a school of thought that says you should always leave people waiting a bit, because this gives the impression that you're important and you are really in demand, and if you reply too fast you are acting a little bit desperate, but in my experience, it's the new client who is desperate, and if you don't reply straight away, they will simply find someone else.

Tip 10

Finally....learn to respect your voice! Get into the habit of drinking a glass of water every hour during the day, eat healthily and exercise daily. Try not to cough to clear your voice, and when you have to shout, either for a voice acting job or if you are in an argument in real life, be aware of the damage this could be doing, so learn the illusionary acting technique for shouting, that "sounds" loud, but isn't actually and won't harm the vocal cords as much.

Thank you for reading and good luck in your own career. More training from myself on voice quality, voice work and software such as adobe audition is at **www.VoiceoverMasterclass.com**

I hope you've found this book useful to you, a review is always welcomed!

Best wishes

Peter Baker

Printed in Great Britain
by Amazon

72745321R00139